INSIGHT GUIDES

Great Breaks

GLASGOW

APA PUBLICATIONS **L**

Part of the Langenscheidt Publishing Group

Contents

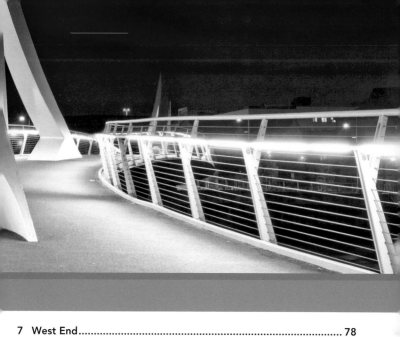

Glasgow's Top 10

From Glasgow's dazzling variety of art and architecture to the wild natural beauty of the surrounding countryside, here, at a glance, are the top sights and activities of this fascinating Scottish city

▲ **Kelvingrove Art Gallery and Museum** *(p.72)*. Discover the wonders of Victorian civic endeavour at this red-sandstone museum filled with compelling exhibits.

▲ **Shopping**. Choose from swanky designers at Princes Square *(p.56)* or quirky boutiques in the Merchant City *(p.45)* and West End *(pp.69 & 83)*.

▲ **Loch Lomond and the Trossachs** *(p.104)*. It's adventures galore in this national park, dipping into Britain's largest lake, trekking and visiting beguiling villages.

▶ **Glasgow culture and nightlife** *(p.10)*. With its myriad music scenes, cutting-edge theatre and nightspots, Glasgow caters for everyone.

▲ **Cathedral and Necropolis** *(pp.20 & 22)*. Glasgow's impressive cathedral was founded in 1136, while the Necropolis provides spine-tingling moments amid crumbling temples and monuments.

▲ **Riverside Museum** *(p.74)*. Glasgow's award-winning new transport museum features buses, trams, trains, bikes and cars.

▲ **Burns Country** *(p.110)*. On the trail of the Scottish bard, visiting Alloway Kirk's graveyard, Burns Cottage, and the Robert Burns Birthplace Museum.

▼ **Pollok Estate** *(p.89)*. A splendid mansion, riverside walks, biking trails, and the world-class Burrell Collection make for a memorable Southside day.

▼ **New Lanark** *(p.109)*. David Dale and his son-in-law Robert Owen's model factory town is now a fascinating Unesco World Heritage Site.

▼ **Glasgow arts scene** *(p.66)*. The Glasgow School of Art and assorted galleries give the city one of the world's most vibrant contemporary art scenes.

The Art of Reinvention

Glasgow is a city continually in flux: its vibrant culture, and its grand architectural splendours of sandstone and steel make it sparkle despite dark urban realities

Glasgow is something of a Renaissance city. Like a proud fighter who refuses to be knocked down, this vibrant, bustling, rumbustious Scottish city is once again busy reinventing itself. Born as a fishing village on the slopes

above the meandering River Clyde, Glasgow has been, in turn, a market town, an ecclesiastical centre, a seat of learning, a city of merchant adventurers, a gateway to the New World, an industrial powerhouse of the British Empire and a European cultural capital.

ARCHITECTURE

Approaching from the south, first impressions are not great. However, despite some misguided 1960s urban planning – Brutalist tower blocks and the M8 motorway which rips through the heart of the city – Glasgow is an architectural treasure house. Its mix of Victorian, Georgian, Venetian and Art Deco equals anything in Europe.

The city retained its grim face until well into the second half of the 20th century, when the New Glasgow Society – a loose collection of early eco-warriors – led a rearguard action against the City Corporation's policy of 'If it's old, knock it down'. Victorian tenement homes were stripped and refurbished instead of being demolished, revealing honey-and-red sandstone wonders and striking detail. The defining moment in Glasgow's recent past was its selection in 1990 as European City of Culture.

ECONOMY AND RENEWAL

Today the city is once again reviving its fortunes with the bold regeneration of the inner-city riverbank. In 2011, the Zaha Hadid-designed Riverside Museum added to the shimmering riverside scene. Meanwhile, the Merchant City's abandoned warehouses continue to be transformed into swanky apartments, businesses and restaurants. The Trongate 103 arts centre is at the centre of a plan to regenerate run-down streets and connect the city with the Clyde.

Glasgow boasts some chic shopping centres, such as Princes Square. High-profile events like the biennial Glasgow International Festival and preparations for the Commonwealth Games in 2014 are reinvigorating the city. Its reputation as a dour, violent slum is finally being shaken off and Glaswegians are generally proud of the transformation.

Above: Glasgow's skyline reveals its rich mix of architectural styles. **Below**: the riverside is packed with striking buildings, such as the Science Centre.

LOCATION

The city lies in the wide strath, or plain, of the River Clyde and is sheltered to the north, east and south by high, open ground; it's possible to be in rolling countryside 20 minutes' drive from the city centre. Glasgow is about 26 miles (40km) from the sea at Greenock, and the Clyde starts to widen into the Firth just below the Erskine Bridge at Old Kilpatrick. North of the city, the Campsie Fells rise to 1,900ft (600m) and are dramatically visible from many areas.

CLIMATE

The Gulf Stream warms the whole of the west coast of Scotland, and Glasgow is a beneficiary of more temperate weather than might be expected from its latitude. Winters are generally mild (between 0°C/32°F and 6°C/43°F) with more rain than snow, though cold snaps of as low as -24°C (-11°F) have been known. Summers, in common with the rest of Britain, appear to be growing warmer, with temperatures of up to 25°C (77°F).

However, the prevailing westerly winds which blow across the Atlantic bring with them their fair share of rain. A day which offers glorious sunshine in the morning can become a depression of drizzle by the early afternoon. Go prepared.

Above: the doomed ocean liner RMS *Lusitania*, pictured here in 1907, was built in the Glasgow shipyards.

Above: the grand Merchants' House (*see p.58*) in 1874.

HISTORY OF TURMOIL

Glasgow was inhabited as long ago as 4000BC, when hunters pushed north in the wake of the retreating ice. Roman general Agricola found hostile tribes in the area in AD80 and threw up a chain of forts across the narrow waist of Scotland. The retreat of the Romans led to centuries of turmoil between warring tribes of Scots, Picts, Britons and Angles.

St Ninian began missionary work in Strathclyde in the 4th century, but St Mungo is credited as the founder of the city in AD543, although only legend bears witness to his arrival. Glasgow Cathedral was founded in 1136 on the site of St Mungo's Church on the banks of the Molendinar, a pretty *burn* (stream). But, although the city was seen as a respectable seat of learning (Glasgow University was created in 1451) with strong religious traditions throughout the Middle Ages, all the political and military action took place in Edinburgh, Falkirk and Stirling.

INDUSTRIAL AWAKENING

The British Empire spawned Glasgow's development as an important port city. John Golborne's ingenious plan of the

F The People

Glaswegians have a way with words, even if visitors have difficulty understanding them. The patter, sociologists argue, is a mix of native sharpness, Highland feyness, Jewish morbidity and the Irish *craic* (witty story-telling). Much of Glasgow's story has been harsh, and, in the past, raising a laugh served as an antidote to adversity. The shipyards of the 1960s, for example, have provided plenty of material for Glaswegian-born comedian, Billy Connolly.

Above: Glaswegians are generally very quick and funny.

1770s – to build piers along the banks and allow the river to scour its own bed – turned Glasgow into a serious contender as an Atlantic port.

The 'Tobacco Lords' were the first major merchants; many of their houses still stand. They created not only the tobacco trade with Maryland, Virginia and North Carolina, but a merchant class. Their need for iron tools, glass, pottery and clothes to trade with the colonies was the impetus for the city's awakening to the Industrial Revolution.

Glasgow became a cotton town in 1780. Within a decade, scores of mills were using the fast-flowing Scottish rivers to power their looms, and immigrants from Ireland and the Highlands were flooding in. Glasgow's population exploded, from 23,500 in 1755 to a peak of 1,128,000 in 1939. The metal-bashing industries – shipbuilding, ironworks, armaments – were complemented by textiles, chemicals and manufacturing.

During the 20th century, Glasgow shared in the spoils and misfortunes of the industrialised world. There may be no more belching foundries or clanging, but recent city administrations have pragmatically courted private finance to unlock the city's post-industrial potential. New developments and attractions are sprouting everywhere, bringing with them a new sense of civic pride. Glasgow is flourishing once again.

Find our recommended restaurants at the end of each Tour. Below is a price guide to help you make your choice.

Eating Out Price Guide

Two-course meal for one person, including a glass of wine.

£££	over £45
££	£25–45
£	under £25

Guide to Coloured Boxes

E Eating	This guide is dotted with coloured boxes providing additional practical and cultural information to make the most of your visit. Here is a guide to the coding system.
F Fact	
G Green	
K Kids	
S Shopping	
V View	

Entertainment

PERFORMING ARTS

Glasgow is a thriving centre for the arts, mixing the old with some of Scotland's most cutting-edge scenes. When it comes to variety of music events, art shows and nightlife, few cities in Britain can compare. For full details of performance times and dates, check in the local press (*The Herald* and *The List* are the best), or visit www.seeglasgow.com.

Theatre, dance, opera and comedy

The Citizens Theatre (tel: 0141-429 0022; www.citz.co.uk) in Gorbals Street combines iconoclastic drama with stunning design. **Tramway** (tel: 0845-330 3501; www.tramway.org) is an exciting arts centre and theatre space, home of Scottish Ballet.

Above: the iconic Clyde Auditorium, popularly known as the Armadillo.

The **Tron Theatre** (tel: 0141-552 4267; www.tron.co.uk) shows hard-hitting Scottish drama, concerts, comedy and pantomime. Comedians Billy Connolly and Dave Gorman appear at **The King's Theatre** (tel: 0844-871 7627) in Bath Street and **Pavilion** in Renfield Street (tel: 0141-332 1846).

Scottish Opera and Scottish Ballet mount major productions at the **Theatre Royal** (tel: 0844-871 7627). Modern dance productions, musicals and plays are also staged here.

Below: the Art Deco Glasgow Film Theatre champions arty fare.

Classical music and gigs

The **Glasgow Royal Concert Hall** (tel: 0141-353 8000) hosts regular performances by the **Royal Scottish National Orchestra** (tel: 0141-225 3561; www.rsno.org.uk). The refurbished **City Halls** and the **Old Fruit Market** in the Merchant City area are home to the **BBC Scottish Symphony Orchestra** and the Scottish Music Centre (tel: 0141-353 8000). **Henry Wood Hall** (tel: 0141-225 3555), at 73 Claremont Street, is a beautiful venue in a former church, mainly used for classical events.

The **Scottish Exhibition and Conference Centre** (tel: 0141-248 3000) and the adjacent **Clyde Auditorium** – dubbed the 'Armadillo'

Tour 1

High Street

This half-day, 1-mile (1.6km) walk takes you from the gritty old traders' hub Mercat Cross up to the spiritual and spooky realms of the Cathedral area and Necropolis

Mercat Cross was the visible evidence of a burgh's right to hold a market, the domain of traders and merchants, making this area Glasgow's traditional centre of social and economic life for many centuries. There is no clear evidence of exactly where the original **Mercat Cross ❶** stood, and the squat octagonal building with a unicorn-topped pillar that now stands on the intersection at Glasgow Cross is a replacement erected in 1929. The Mercat Building located behind it is, despite its Chicagoesque appearance, a warehouse erected in 1925. The new arts centre Trongate 103 and the Tron theatre *(see p.41 for both)* are slowly revitalising this part of the Merchant City area.

Highlights

- Tolbooth Steeple
- Barony Hall
- Provand's Lordship
- St Mungo Museum of Religious Life and Art
- Glasgow Cathedral
- Necropolis

TOLBOOTH STEEPLE

Starting our walk here, the cross is dominated by the **Tolbooth Steeple ❷**, which lies stranded in the middle of busy traffic where the High Street passes into Saltmarket. The Tolbooth was once an integral part of civic life in Glasgow and has occupied this site in various forms since the earliest days. Its on the right. The street names offer clues to the past: Blackfriars Street, from the 13th-century Dominican monastery; Bell Street, after Provost Sir John Bell (1680); and College Street, denoting the **Old College** which was sited here until the middle of the 19th century. The University of Glasgow was established by Bishop William Turnbull in 1451 and flourished for the next few centuries in a pleasant environment between the High Street and the Molendinar Burn. It was here that Adam Smith, author of seminal work on laissez-faire economics *The Wealth of Nations*, was appointed Professor of Moral Philosophy in 1752.

The university moved westwards in 1870 (see p.80), and the site was sold to the City of Glasgow Union Railway Company, which demolished it and erected the College Goods Station, which has now also gone. However, the area is currently undergoing substantial redevelopment.

Preceding Pages: Bells Bridge and the 'Armadillo'. **Left:** the Necropolis. **Above:** the Tolbooth Steeple.

functions were manifold, from a meeting place for the town council, to a tax collection point, courthouse and jail.

The square tower was part of a five-storey building which extended west along the Trongate, towards the steeple of **Tron-St Mary's** (see p.41), and its buttressed crown houses the latest of a fine carillon of bells which, in the 18th century, played out a different Scottish melody every two hours. The present bells, installed in 1881, were tended by hereditary bell-ringers, the last of whom, Jessie Herbert, rang the bells until 1970. Their annual high point was, of course, marking the Hogmanay celebrations which saw vast crowds welcoming the New Year in boisterous fashion. The Hogmanay party now takes place in George Square, to the sound of rock bands.

HISTORICAL HIGH STREET

The High Street runs north past Victorian tenements (1883), with shops below on the left and new flats converted from old warehouses

Above: Barony Hall was designed in the Scottish Gothic Revival style and is a popular venue for weddings, as well as the site of graduation ceremonies.

On the left, opposite the High Street Station, is the shell of the old **British Linen Bank**, which has a statue of Pallas, goddess of wisdom and weaving, and a plaque on the corner recalling that the poet Thomas Campbell frequented a coffee shop on the site. Close by, on Nicholas Street, is the Old College Bar, Glasgow's most ancient pub (est. 1515).

Crossing George Street and curving up the hill, the street is flanked by restored tenements with crow-stepped gables, turrets and balconies. On this hill, the Scots freedom fighter William Wallace – glorified by Hollywood and Mel Gibson in the film *Braveheart* – fought a running battle with English forces in 1297.

UNIVERSITY DIGS

On the corner of High Street and Rottenrow is **Barony Hall ❸** (Sat–Sun), the first major building of the Cathedral complex, which opens out onto Castle Street. It was built in 1889 from beautiful red sandstone and graced with slender stained-glass windows and a grey Gothic spire. It is now owned by

the University of Strathclyde, and on graduation days the street teems with begowned students and tutors making their way to the hall to receive and bestow degrees. Rottenrow is one of Glasgow's earliest streets, and its name has never been adequately defined,

Below: the Mercat Building *(see p.14)* on the Trongate.

with suggestions as far apart as *route du roi* (king's way) to *vicus ratonum* (street of rats). It leads to the university's **Campus Village** ❹, a pleasing and colourful student quarter built over the past two decades, proving that not all modern architecture is unsympathetic.

AROUND CATHEDRAL SQUARE

Opposite Barony Hall is **Cathedral Square** ❺, guarded by a rather imperious equestrian statue of William of Orange, which was resited by the Provincial Grand Black Chapter of Scotland in 1989 from the Trongate, where it suffered terrible indignities each Hogmanay. It is said that the tail of King Billy's horse was broken off by a reveller and replaced with a ball and socket joint, with the result that on particularly stormy days, the tail can be seen to wave in the breeze.

On the south side of the square is the 1960s Ladywell housing estate, built over the medieval well of that name and the former Duke Street jail. The east side is bounded by the **Glasgow Evangelical Church** ❻, which features life-sized statues of the Apostles. Just to the north, more worldly pleasures can be found at the **Cathedral House**, a small hotel housed in a red sandstone building dating from 1896, which has an interesting three-level bar and is reputedly haunted.

The oldest dwelling-house still standing in Glasgow is **Provand's Lordship** ❼ (tel: 0141-552 8819; www.glasgowlife.org.uk; Tue–Thur, Sat 10am–5pm, Fri–Sun 11am–5pm; free). It lies opposite Cathedral Square and was built in 1471 by Bishop Andrew Muirhead to house the master of the hospice of St Nicholas, who looked after a complement of 12 old men.

The house was saved and restored in 1906, with financial aid and period furnishings supplied by Sir William

Above: a sign indicates the oldest Glasgow house still standing, Provand's Lordship, which is now a museum portraying medieval life in the city.

ⓕ Gruesome Tales

If spirits haunt any part of Glasgow, it should be here. Men and women were hanged outside the Tolbooth, and alleged witches and miscreants scourged. The original building had spikes on the walls for the decapitated heads of felons. When the justiciary decamped to the river end of the Saltmarket and the council moved west, the main part of the Tolbooth was lost; only the steeple and its winding stone staircase remain.

Above: the Tolbooth has a long and gruesome history.

Burrell (see p.90) in 1927, and is now run by Glasgow Museums. Behind it lies a **Physic Garden**, in tribute to St Nicholas. The sound of the traffic gives way to medieval calm here, among the herb plantings and knot gardens. Behind the wall, towards the Strathclyde campus, is a small but ambitious orchard, where students convene under the spring blossom and try to ignore the M8 just up the road.

RELIGION AND MEDICINE

Back across the High Street – traffic is always bad here – is the **St Mungo Museum of Religious Life and Art** ❽ (tel: 0141-276 1625; www.glasgowlife.org.uk; Tue–Thur, Sat 10am–5pm; Fri and Sun 11am–5pm; free), which caused some controversy before it was opened in 1993 over whether it was an architectural pastiche. The honey-coloured stone building stands on the site of the medieval Bishop's Castle and houses works of art from the main religions – Buddhist, Christian, Hindu, Jewish, Muslim and Sikh – as well as minor ones. Religious rites are explained alongside intriguing relics and there are gorgeous views from the top floor.

Above: a restored room at Provand's Lordship depicts medieval living.

Inside the Gallery of Religious Art there are powerful images of religious figures and rites to explore, including an imposing figure of the Hindu god Shiva, Lord of the Dance, and the Mexican Day of the Dead skeleton, which celebrates the victory of life over death. Illuminating the poignant images are some truly stunning stained-glass windows showing Christian saints and prophets. The museum's pleasant coffee shop backs onto an attractive Zen-style garden

Ⓢ Quirky Shops on the High Street

Along this sweep of handsome red-brick tenements – between the pubs and fish-and-chip takeaways – there are dishevelled shopfronts aplenty. But tucked in among the intriguing and slightly unsettling array of shops – from beauty/massage parlours and hairdressers to religious missions and a butcher or two – lies **23enigma** (258 High Street; tel: 0141-553 1990), bubbling with spell books, talismans and crystals. It even offers alternative therapies including hypnosis and reiki.

Above: tarot cards are just some of the spooky wares on offer at 23enigma.

Above: the St Mungo Museum of Religious Life and Art has won awards for its fascinating exhibits and attempts to promote inter-faith understanding.

designed by Yasutaro Tanaka, another unexpected haven of peace in this busy street.

The cathedral precinct is fronted by a statue of the Scots missionary explorer David Livingstone *(see p.107)* and provides an excellent foreground for the massive bulk of the **Royal Infirmary ❾**, which was completed in 1915 and commemorates the 65-year reign of Queen Victoria, whose solemn presence looms above the entrance. The Royal, which has been operating since 1794, has made a proud contribution to world medicine: Lord Lister pioneered antiseptic surgery here in the 1860s; Sir William Macewen established his reputation in brain surgery and osteopathy here in the 1890s; and his matron Mrs Rebecca Strong introduced the world's first systematic training for nurses. In the early part of the 19th century, its resources were considerably stretched as it sought to cope with epidemics of cholera, typhus

Above: the Royal Infirmary has been the site of many medical breakthroughs.

Above: Barony Chapel, in the crypt of Glasgow Cathedral, is so named because it was used by Barony parishioners for their worship.

and dysentery. Today, it has one of the busiest casualty departments in Europe, coping with Glasgow's still prevalent weekend bouts of random and inventive violence. One casualty surgeon remarked that it was one of the few cities in Europe where patients still came in with sword wounds.

GLASGOW CATHEDRAL

At the east end of the precinct lies **Glasgow Cathedral** ❿ (tel: 0141-552 8198; Apr–Sept Mon–Sat 9.30am–5.30pm, Sun 1–5pm, Oct–Mar Mon–Sat 9.30am–4.30pm, Sun 1–4.30pm). The tides of history have washed over this important ecclesiastical site since Glasgow's early days. It was founded in 1136 on the site of St Mungo's Church and has always been a focus for Christian learning and culture in Scotland. It has stood through the supremacy of the bishops, the War of Independence and the upheaval of the Reformation, and began to take the shape

which we see today around the middle of the 14th century. Its blackened stone illustrates the colouring of many Glasgow buildings before stone-cleaning became widespread.

Below: Glasgow Cathedral is the best-preserved medieval church in Scotland.

Above: the cathedral is known for its magnificent stained-glass windows.

culture of the operative classes'. The grounds are surrounded by gravestones. Blue-robed custodians belonging to the Society of Friends of Glasgow Cathedral give fascinating little impromptu tours.

Music enthusiasts and anyone interested in the labyrinthine history of this colossal building will be keen to find out about the latest recitals and lectures held in the cathedral. Completing the warm welcome given to visitors and incredible resources available to the curious, there is the Congregations' Library, which is situated in the Cathedral Hall in the basement of the nearby St Mungo Museum (see p.18). It is open on Wednesday afternoons from 2pm to 4pm.

Attempts have been made to clean it up, but it was felt that it would cause too much damage.

The visitors' entrance is flanked by a memorial to the Hutcheson brothers and George Baillie, who 'divested himself of his fortune to endow institutions devoted to the intellectual

Architectural features

The main structure is a rectangle with a cross surmounted by a tower and steeple. A lower church opens up underneath the choir. Damaged by fire, the original cathedral building was succeeded by a larger one, which was consecrated in 1197. Major 13th-century rebuilding by William de Bondinton (1233–58) can be seen in the Quire and the Lower

F St Mungo

Legend has it that a century after St Ninian dedicated a Christian burial ground at Cathures (later Glasgow) Kentigern arrived, popularly known as Mungo. Kentigern hailed from Culross in Fife (Glaswegians may be taken aback to learn that their patron saint was in fact a Fifer) where he was trained as a priest by St Serf. He accompanied the corpse of a holy man, Fergus – carried on a cart by two oxen – to the St Ninian's burial ground in Cathures where Fergus was buried.

Above: images of St Mungo, Glasgow's patron saint, adorn the city.

Church. Check out the doorways of the sacristy (Upper Chapterhouse) and of the Lower Chapterhouse; these date from the mid-13th century. Extensive work enlarged the nave in the 14th century – for a closer look at these developments seek out the southwest door and the entrance to the Blacader Aisle, where the body of Fergus is said to have been buried by St Mungo *(see box p.21)*.

Other intriguing architectural and social developments occurred after the Reformation to allow three different congregations to worship in different spaces, reflecting rank and class divisions. From 1595, the Barony Parishioners worshipped in the lower church (crypt), while from 1648 the High Kirk congregation worshipped in the choir itself, and the nave was used by worshippers from the eastern part of the city. Ask one of the robed custodians for interesting tidbits from this period.

NECROPOLIS

At the south side of the Cathedral is a bridge which spans Wishart Street and leads to the **Necropolis** ⓫ (7am–dusk; free) an impressive ornamental garden cemetery modelled on Père-

Lachaise in Paris. It is full of crumbling temples and monuments, many of which are in a sorry state of repair, which only adds to the chilling atmosphere, especially on dreich days.

In 1831, John Strang, Chamberlain at the Merchants' House, wrote *Necropolis Glasguensis* ('Thoughts on Death and Moral Stimulus'), which included an outline of city plans for the hilly site that had been previously known as Fir Park, which he considered to appear 'admirably

ⓥ Views Between the Tombs

The splendid views from the hill housing the Necropolis not only give some idea of the imposing grandeur of the Cathedral in medieval times, but also stretch as far as Ben Lomond to the north-west and the Cathkin Braes to the south. Roe deer can be seen roaming between the monument obelisks and haughty headstones. The combination of wildlife and monumental Victorian display and decay – with a skyline backdrop of lines of high-rise flats and churches – is strangely spine-tingling.

Above: situated on a hill, the Necropolis offers wonderful views.

Above: crumbling memorials in the Victorian Necropolis.

adapted for a Pere la Chaise, which would harmonise beautifully with the adjacent scenery, and constitute a solemn and appropriate append-age to the venerable structure (the Cathedral) in front of which, while it will afford a much wanted ac-commodation to the higher classes, would at the same time convert an

Below: a Celtic cross adorns a grave in the Necropolis.

unproductive property into a gen-eral and lucrative source of profit, to a charitable institution'. It was to be 'respectful to the dead, safe and sanitary to the living, dedicated to the Genius of Memory and to extend religious and moral feeling'.

Architect David Hamilton, Stuart Murray, Curator of the Botanic Gar-dens, and James Clelland, Superintend-ent of Public Works, produced a fea-sibility study for forming the Glasgow Necropolis, and in 1828 the commit-tee of Directors of Lands and Quar-ries agreed to the proposal. Then in 1831, a competition for converting the Fir Park into a cemetery was launched, with five prizes up for grabs of £10–50. As the burial ground was intended to be interdenominational, the first burial in 1832 was fittingly that of a Jew, Joseph Levi, a jeweller. Extensions into quarry ground in the 1860s and 1870s give us the present-day dimen-sions of 37 acres (15 hectares).

A walk around the graves
Some 50,000 burials have taken place at the Necropolis and most of the 3,500 tombs are about 14ft (4m)

Above: one of the Necropolis's elaborate tombs.

deep, with solid stone walls and brick partitions. Some of the Necropolis tombs on the top of the hill were blasted out of the rock face. Many of the monuments were designed by major architects and sculptors, including Alexander 'Greek' Thomson, Charles Rennie Mackintosh and

Below: a stone angel on one of the Necropolis's monuments.

J.T. Rochead, which makes a walk around the sprawling site a fascinating insight into both Victorian and Edwardian styles and tastes. The administration and maintenance of the Necropolis was handed from Merchants' House to Glasgow City Council in 1966.

The Necropolis's grand bridge was built by the Merchants' House of Glasgow to 'afford a proper entrance to the new cemetery combining convenient access to the grounds' and views of 'the venerable Cathedral and surrounding scenery'. Paths lead in circles round the hill past gloomy, ivy-clad, marble-pillared tombs and sombre obelisks. The Victorians took themselves as seriously in death as in life. The crowning monument on the summit is to John Knox, the austere father of the Reformation in Scotland, which 'produced a revolution in the sentiments of mankind'. Knox still keeps a suspicious eye on the city below. The Friends of Glasgow Necropolis (www. glasgownecropolis.org) is a superb organisation which runs tours of the site and various cultural events.

BACK TO GLASGOW CROSS

Leaving the cemetery in Wishart Street, this tour continues past the huge steel tanks of the **Tennent Caledonian Brewery**, which supplies a commodity as welcome to many Glaswegians as Loch Katrine's water. At the foot of the street the modern flats and high-rise blocks on the right stand on the site of the Drygate, one of the original streets of old Glasgow.

Turning right into Duke Street, past the former Alexander's School, now a business centre (adorned with busts of the heads of Shakespeare and other luminaries on its frontage), the road follows along the wall of the old College Goods Yard.

To return to Glasgow Cross, turn left at the traffic lights and head into the High Street.

Above: the tanks of the Tennent Caledonian Brewery stand in close proximity to the Necropolis tombs.

E Eating Out

Babbity Bowsters
16–18 Blackfriars Street; tel: 0141-552 5055; daily lunch and dinner.
Housed in a handsome Adam brothers-designed building, this popular hangout has the Schottische restaurant serving hearty portions of Scottish classic dishes with a Gallic twist here and there. The homely pub serves decent ales and malts to a live folk music soundtrack. This place is popular with a diverse crowd. £

St Mungo Museum Café
St Mungo Museum of Religious Life and Art; Tue–Thur, Sat 10am–5pm, Fri and Sun 11am–5pm.
This museum café serves predominantly simple, honest British grub, as well as some pasta dishes, heaped salads and good-value soup of the day. There is also an attractive garden where you can enjoy your meal in good weather. £

Above: Babbity Bowsters.

Tour 2

The Barras to Saltmarket

This short 2-mile (3.2km) walk takes in the banter and bargains of the Barras, Glasgow Green's delights and a short stroll south to the Clyde

If the High Street walk (see p.14) uncovers layers of Glasgow's history, this tour, which takes in the lively Barras, is where the city's working class past meets modern struggles and endeavours. This walk is a real eye-opener and is bound to deliver some memorable, oddball stories, encounters and scenes.

Although at first glance this busy marketplace is tatty and run-down, the area is full of life and colour, and bargain-hunters flock to it from all over the city and beyond. Down towards the Clyde and over the bridge there are old and new popular Glaswegian institutions – including the People's Palace museum and the handsome Winter Gardens at Glasgow Green – as well as the Citizens Theatre and

Central Mosque. Round the corner from historic folk music pubs there are notorious locations etched on the Glaswegian psyche, like Nelson's Pillar, sight of many a public hanging.

Left: one of the riverside developments on the banks of the Clyde. **Above:** the Central Mosque *(see p.34)*.

Saturday or Sunday are the best days to undertake this tour, as the majority of shops around the Saltmarket are open.

ALONG GALLOWGATE

Starting the walk from the **Mercat Cross** *(see p.14)*, head east up the **Gallowgate**, which is generally accepted to have the macabre meaning

its name implies. However, the late historian George Eyre-Todd suggested that it meant the *gait*, or way to, the *gia lia*, or sacred stone of Celtic times, which would make it one of the oldest roads in Scotland. Social raconteur Jack House recalls days in the 1930s when the street housed 60 pubs and he 'never ventured there without an occasional *frisson* disturbing me'.

The road leads under a bridge, passing a row of discount shops, as well as Moir Street and Charlotte Street, after which you reach Glasgow's oldest chippie (1884) at Little Dovehill and then Great Dovehill on the left. According to legend, this is where St Mungo was preaching to his flock when someone at the back complained that he could not see him, whereupon he commanded the adjoining ground to rise up in the air.

A little further along, you will come to **The Saracen's Head ❶** (Sat 11am–11pm, Sun 12.30–11pm), or 'The Sarry Heid', a pub whose glory days are most definitely behind it. It lays claim to being the first real hotel in Glasgow, built in 1755 from the ruins of the old bishop's castle, and takes its name from a 12th-century

Above: the Barras market takes its name from the Glaswegian dialect for 'barrow'; in the market's early years, the traders sold their goods from handcarts.

inn in London frequented by Richard the Lionheart. The first mail coach from London arrived here in 1788, and it was a haunt of Scotland's judges as they progressed round the western circuit from Edinburgh.

THE BARRAS

Crossing the road to Kent Street, **The Barras** ❷ (Sat–Sun 10am–5pm) originated as a street market consisting of hand-barrows hired out by the McIver family to traders too poor to have their own. The covered market came into being in 1926 and, after a spell in the doldrums in the 1970s and 1980s, it has been revitalised and is now said to be one of the biggest markets in Europe.

Second-hand furniture and clothes predominate, although in keeping with the times, DVDs, computer games and CDs, whose legality is continually challenged by trading standards officers, now feature. Slightly further along the Gallowgate from the Kent Street entrance is the **Barrowland Ballroom**, a dance

Ⓕ Sarry Heid's Colourful Patrons and Relics

The old inn has been visited by an impressive list of patrons, including Robert Burns, John Wesley, James Boswell, William Wordsworth and Adam Smith, who was allegedly ejected after a swearing match with Dr Samuel Johnson. It houses the 1760 Saracen's Head punchbowl and the skull of Maggie, the last witch to be burned at the stake, which the title deeds demand is to be passed to the People's Palace if the pub is ever demolished.

Glasgow's first
PUB - MUSEUM

See the 'Skull of Maggie' the last witch to be burned at the stake. Read a poem in Rabbie Burns' ane handwriting.

Above: the Sarry Heid's inn displays a range of quirky artefacts.

Above: the Barrowland Ballroom is a popular venue with a variety of local and high-profile international acts, who praise the acoustics and atmosphere.

hall which was the focus of the 1960s Bible John murders – when three women were killed by a man with a penchant for quoting Old Testament texts to his victims – but is now one of Glasgow's largest live music venues, staging gigs by local bands like Camera Obscura and international stars, including one of Dumbarton's finest sons, David Byrne.

In case you are wondering about the green-and-white-striped men often seen staggering along the Gallowgate, chanting musical ditties, these are fans of Celtic Football Club. Among the many bars to and from **Celtic Park Stadium**, a 15-minute walk east of the Barras, is Baird's Bar, next door to the Barrowland

Ballroom. It is a well-known Hoops haunt and pre-gig watering hole. Pop your head in to see an eye-opening afternoon karaoke session, or if you are on the way to a game at Paradise, Celtic's home ground (for fixtures and tickets go to www.celticfc.net), this is a good spot to soak up some local banter and gauge the mood of the local support.

Kent Street leads through to London Road, and, turning left, you'll see St Alphonsus Church. Next door is **Glasgow Antiques Market** (tel: 0141-552 6989; Sat–Sun 9.30am–4.30pm), which has a café attached. Proceed down Bain Street, through the Maggie McIvers Gate, and into **Glasgow Green**. Through the trees you will see the exotic coloured-brick frontage of the old Templeton's carpet factory, an enthusiastic copy of the Doge's Palace in Venice, designed by William Leiper in 1889. The factory is now a business centre.

PEOPLE'S PALACE

Turn left for the **People's Palace ❸** (tel: 0141-276 0788; www.glasgow life.org.uk; Tue–Thur and Sat 10am–5pm, Fri and Sun 11am–5pm; free), a museum presiding over one of the

Left: shopping for fruit and veg at the Barras; a farmers' market is also held here on the last Saturday of the month.

tree-lined avenues of Glasgow Green and a favourite with Glaswegians. It was built as a cultural centre for workers in 1898, who were living in some of the most abject conditions of the Industrial age. Lord Rosebery outlined the purpose of the grandiose civic project: 'A palace of pleasure and imagination around which the people may place their affections and which may give them a home on which their memory may rest'. He then declared the building as 'Open to the people for ever and ever'.

Originally, the ground floor provided space for reading and recreation, with a museum on the first floor, and a picture gallery on the top floor. Since the 1940s it has concentrated on the history and the way of life of the working class as well as kings and cardinals. Exhibits range from a ring that belonged to Mary, Queen of Scots to comedian Billy Connolly's 'banana boots'. The

Above: an exotic and colourful flower at the Winter Gardens.

red-sandstone building, with its domed roof and pillared frontage, was completely refurbished for its centenary in 1998 and now uses the latest computer technology and film to tell its story.

On the top floor is a powerful series of paintings by artist and Glasgow

Above: the Winter Gardens hosts exhibitions and events throughout the year.

Above: the Winter Gardens café is a pleasant place to spend some time, particularly on a cold or rainy day.

School of Art graduate Ken Currie, who was commissioned to mark the 1987 bicentenary of the massacre of Glasgow's Calton weavers, Scotland's first trade union martyrs. The series of eight paintings adorns the splendid dome: the cycle begins in 1787 and ends with a vision of the future. It traces the development of the Scottish labour movement through Currie's powerful imagery. **The Winter Gardens** (daily 10am–5pm), a huge conservatory housing tropical palms and ferns, butts onto the back of the Palace. After a serious fire in 1998, it has now reopened and houses a café-cum-bar.

GLASGOW GREEN

In 1450 Bishop Turnbull gave the common lands of **Glasgow Green** to the people of the city, although its previously rural vista is now bounded by the high-rise flats of the Gorbals, across the river. Bonnie Prince Charlie mustered his armies here, and the Glasgow Fair, instituted in 1190, is still celebrated in the park in the last fortnight of July. Turning right past the palace, a 144ft (44m) needle erected to commemorate Lord Nelson dominates the western end.

In front of the People's Palace, the magnificent red-terracotta **Doulton Fountain ❹**, gifted by the Victorian china manufacturer to commemorate Queen Victoria's Golden Jubilee of 1887, has recently been restored with investment from the National Lottery Fund. Its five-tier, 46ft (14m) -high and 70ft (21m) -wide display of imperial pride makes it the largest terracotta fountain in the world and a mesmerising insight into Glasgow's prominent place in the British Empire. It was first unveiled at the Empire Exhibition held at Kelvingrove Park in 1888 and then moved to Glasgow Green in 1890. Walk around it to get a closer look at extravagant figurative groups representing India, Australia,

Saturdays @ the Palace

On selected Saturdays, usually once a month, at 2pm the People's Palace holds a family-friendly event that is aimed at entertaining and engaging children with the museum's exhibits. The talks are often themed, from the history of World War II to Scottish royalty, or may reflect the time of year, such as a day of Halloween fun.

Above: the splendid People's Palace and Doulton Fountain on Glasgow Green.

Canada and South Africa. Seek out national flora and fauna (South Africa's ostrich, Australian sheep and Canadian beaver), alongside military and naval figures including a kilted highlander. Completing the array of dizzying decorations are gargoyles, coats of arms, lion masks, and young girls pouring water over the figures below. Topping the whole Imperial enterprise is a lifelike statue of Queen Victoria.

Ⓢ Independent Shopping

It may have the Barras and some scruffy old markets, but this area is not renowned for its upmarket shopping. However, a few excellent independent shops and specialist outlets have opened in recent years which are well worth seeking out. **Monorail** (12 Kings Court, King Street; tel: 0141-553 2400; Mon–Sat 11am–7pm, Sun noon–5pm) is run by Pastels front man Stephen Pastel, and is a must for musos and vinyl addicts. They have a great vegan-friendly café and a space for cultural events, cinema screenings and other cultural get-togethers.

Just north of Monorail is Glasgow's best comic shop, **A1 Comics** (35 Parnie Street; tel: 0141-552 6692; daily 9.30am–5.30pm, Sun noon–5pm), which has some fine toys for kids and objects for geeky adults alongside piles of Marvel and DC editions. Just off the London Road is **GOOD:D** (11 James Morrison Street; tel: 0141-552 6777; daily 9.30am–5.30pm, Sun noon–5pm), which is full of quirky modern design pieces.

Above: the music shop Monorail is heaven for vinyl lovers.

Above: Nelson's Pillar (1806) was the first civic monument in Britain to commemorate the Admiral's victories.

ST ANDREW'S IN THE SQUARE

Returning north to London Road, along Charlotte Street, is Glickman's fabulous confectionery shop (est. 1903), a sweet-tooth's paradise. The tour continues towards Glasgow Cross and left into James Morrison Street and St Andrew's Square, which is home to **St Andrew's Parish Church ❺** (now known as St Andrew's in the Square), the oldest church in the city after the Cathedral. It was modelled on St Martin-in-the-Fields in London, and its massive pillars and stone ornamentation illustrate the grand tastes of the 18th-century Tobacco Lords. It now stages musical and other cultural events, and houses the excellent Café Source (see p.37).

The south side of the square passes the district courts, where minor offenders are daily chastised, and, turning left and then right into Steel Street, the route leads to the Saltmarket. The pub on the facing corner, **The Old Ship Bank**, recalls the first Glasgow bank, set up in 1750 to meet the needs of the influential and rising merchant class. Going left down the Saltmarket, the new **High Court of Justiciary** extension is tucked into Jocelyn Square behind the old Mortuary. Further along is the old High Court, with its forbidding grey-pillared portico, which has seen the black cap donned for a procession of murderers. It fronted onto Jail Square, where the guilty were hanged before cheering crowds in the shadow of Nelson's Pillar, giving rise to the maternal Glaswegian warning to recalcitrant children: 'You'll die facing the monument.'

TOWARDS AND OVER THE CLYDE

Saltmarket runs down onto the **Albert Bridge**, or Hutchesontown Bridge, a cast-iron structure built in 1871 on enormous granite piers on the site of a crossing first created in 1794. Just upstream is the weir which marks the tidal limit of the river and

Above: St Andrew's in the Square has been restored to its 18th-century glory.

Above: inside the Citizens Theatre.

controls its natural vagaries. Over the bridge, appropriately at the river's junction with the sea, is what was the **Glasgow College of Nautical Studies**, which merged with the City of Glasgow College in 2010.

Turning right onto the south bank of the river at the start of the college, a tree-lined walkway leads to the peaceful colonnaded grounds of the **Central Mosque** ❻ (tel: 0141-429 3132; www.centralmosque.co.uk; daily 9am–5pm for visitors, booking essential; 24 hours for prayers), which in 1984 became the first purpose-built mosque in Scotland and is now one of the largest in Europe. Its green, multi-faceted dome and soaring minaret combine Islamic architecture with traditional Scottish sandstone. It provides the facilities of worship for 2,000 Muslims, a community whose numbers have increased dramatically in the 1980s and 1990s and who now play an integral part in city life.

The forbidding black-and-grey-marbled building on the other side of Gorbals Street is the **Sheriff Court** where solicitors gather to ply an ancient trade. It moved here when the old, smaller, city-centre

court became unable to cope with the numbers that make it the busiest court in Europe.

Further south down Gorbals Street, across the junction with Ballater Street, is the **Citizens Theatre** ❼ (tel: 0141-429 0022; www.citz.co.uk), a cornerstone of Glasgow's artistic life and a major contributor to its ambition to be considered as a European city. The Citizen's Company was established in 1943 amid a row of Gorbals tenements, in a grand Victorian

Ⓖ Clyde Walkway

This 40-mile (65km) -long path has been developed to link Glasgow with the Falls of Clyde at Lanark. Cyclists and walkers will particularly enjoy the Glasgow section between Victoria Bridge and the SECC, which passes the PS *Waverley* Terminal – home of the world's last sea-going paddle steamer – and the colossal 176ft (53m) -high Finnieston Crane, which once raised railway locomotives. There are a number of other long-distance paths that link up with the Clyde Walkway, including the Kelvin Walkway, the Glasgow to Inverness National Cycle Route, and paths to Edinburgh, Greenock and Irvine.

Above: see ongoing riverside development from the Clyde Walkway.

building originally called His Majesty's Theatre, which had been opened in 1878. Scottish playwright James Bridie drove the project as part of a plan to establish a Scottish national theatre. It drifted from drama into crisis until the arrival in 1969 of director Giles Havergal and his flamboyant designer Philip Prowse. Their ground-breaking productions – sometimes shocking and disturbing – attracted headlines and interest far beyond Glasgow and continue to fill the hall. The theatre houses a main auditorium and two small studio theatres which offer cutting-edge works.

Below: the Albert Bridge.

Above: Gothic-spired St Andrew's Cathedral is now dwarfed among the modern riverside buildings.

HEADING BACK NORTH OF THE CLYDE

Returning along Gorbals Street, the road comes to **Victoria Bridge**, where the city's first river crossing, a wooden structure commissioned by Bishop Rae in 1350, stood for 450 years. The present bridge is faced

Below: the Clutha Vaults pub is renowned for its live acoustic and folk music and is a real Glasgow institution.

with Dublin granite and affords excellent views down river past the Carlton Place Suspension Bridge to the Jamaica Street and Central Station bridges. The Gothic-spired building on the north bank is **St Andrew's Cathedral** (www.cathedralg1.org; daily 8.15am–5.45pm), the main Roman Catholic church, which is reflected in the modern glass-walled diocesan headquarters next door. The cathedral reopened in 2011 after a substantial renovation and includes a new baptismal font and a new artwork of St Andrew and the city's patron saint St Mungo. The glass pyramids rising above the rooftops behind it are the canopies of the St Enoch shopping centre.

Across the bridge on the north bank, two adjoining pubs, the **Clutha Vaults** and the **Scotch Corner** (both 11am–midnight), may look a tad scruffy from the outside but are a focus for the folk circuit. Above these pubs is the three-tiered spire of the old fish market, topped with a golden sailing ship. Nearby, the Scotia Bar at 112–114 Stockwell Street stages folk acts as well as poetry and literary events.

Under the railway bridge, on waste ground between St Margaret's Place and the new High Court buildings, is where **Paddy's Market** was held until May 2009. The defunct market had its origins, as the name suggests, in the floods of refugees from the Irish potato famine. Labelled a 'crime-ridden midden' by the council, the area is set to be transformed into a new cultural quarter to link up with the exciting new artsy venues and bars on the Trongate and Merchant City *(see p.40)*. Some residents have not taken too kindly to the attempt to gentrify the area, but most see the benefits of encouraging new initiatives to clean up and hopefully transform squalor into a bustling centre of arts and enterprise.

Turning left at the end of the Briggait, the **Saltmarket** – so named because the original market for salt for curing river salmon was here – curves back up to the High Street past restored tenements and busy shops.

A NEW CULTURAL QUARTER

Veering right into the Bridgegate, or Briggait, one of Glasgow's oldest streets, this tour passes second-hand shops, cheap restaurants and the expanse of the King Street car park.

Ⓔ Eating Out

Café Source
1 St Andrew's Square; tel: 0141-548 6020; daily lunch and dinner.
Locally sourced ingredients go into the hearty fare served in the basement of St Andrew's in the Square. £

Maggie May's
60 Trongate; tel: 0141-548 1350; daily lunch and dinner.
Hidden in the back of the busy Maggie's Bar on the Trongate, this intimate place concentrates on traditional Scots fare with some imaginative additions. Standouts include cullen skink, a potato and smoked haddock soup, and crème brulée. £

Mono
12 King's Court, King Street; tel: 0141-553 2400; www.monocafebar.com; Sun–Thur noon–8pm, Fri–Sat noon–10pm; bar noon–midnight, noon–1am Fri–Sat.

A popular music and arts venue with a great record shop, Mono also squeezes in a café with a vegan menu. Top dishes include the falafel platter served with vegetables and hummous, and the Mono veggie burger. £

Above: Café Source offers a range of traditional and modern Scottish fare.

Sandstone & Steel

Roads, slum clearances, high-rise schemes and recession may have savaged the city in the past, but Glasgow's innovative spirit is reinvigorating the urban landscape

SOLID SANDSTONE SPIRIT

In Glasgow's city centre, grand drama and extravagance in sculpted stone predominates.

From the weathered 13th-century remnants found in the vicinity of Glasgow Cathedral and the 17th-century mercantile optimism around the Trongate, to the grandeur of the mansions of the Tobacco Lords in the Merchant City in the 18th century and the robust flowering of the Victorians in the British Empire's heyday, Glasgow developed into a city carved painstakingly from sandstone.

Although Charles Rennie Mackintosh *(see Tour 9)* and Alexander 'Greek' Thomson are foremost in the current view of Glasgow's architectural heritage, others such as William Young – who created the City Chambers as a monument to civic pride in 1888 – J.T. Rochead, J.J. Burnet and Charles Wilson all contributed mightily. Rochead's work in St Vincent Street sets the tone for the commercial centre, and his Grosvenor Hotel is a true Venetian marvel, Burnet's former TSB banking hall on the corner of Ingram Street and Glassford small-scale confections like James Miller's miniature version of France's Azay-le-Rideau in the centre of St Enoch Square.

GLASS, STEEL AND THE FUTURE

Modern architecture in Glasgow is following a bold tradition. Atlantic Quay on the Clyde has waterfront grandeur, as does the Clyde Auditorium (dubbed the Armadillo for its distinctive shape) by Sir Norman Foster. The Glasgow Science Centre complex has titanium curves and a soaring viewing tower, called the Titan. The open-plan interior of the new BBC Scotland building on Pacific Quay is equally bold; so, too, is the Clyde Arc Bridge.

Other visionary projects include the striking Riverside Museum, designed by Zaha Hadid, with its wave-like 'pleated' aluminium shapes, and the new Glasgow School of Art Garnethill Estate redevelopment, opposite Mackintosh's architectural masterpiece is due for completion in 2013. In September 2009, Steven Holl Architects' (New York) light-filled design won a high-profile competition to build the GSA's new teaching and research centre.

Other recent projects have imaginatively adapted some of Glasgow's old sandstone architecture. To the innovative renovations at the Italian Centre, Tron Theatre and Princes Square can be added Trongate 103, a cutting-edge arts hub hewn out of an Edwardian warehouse. It's all part of Glasgow City Council's plan to regenerate this part of the Merchant City down to the River Clyde, and in doing so create an enlarged cultural quarter.

A great way to absorb Glasgow's architecture is on a guided tour. For information about Glasgow Architectural Walking Tours, including a visit to the GSA, check out www.glasgow architecture.co.uk.

Street outshines the bigger surroundings, while Wilson created an Italianate skyscape in the Park Circus area which is unequalled in Britain.

Huge enterprises like Robert Anderson's Central Hotel and the Edwardian mass of the Royal Technical College (now the University of Strathclyde) vie for attention amongst

Above: Tradeston Bridge in Atlantic Quay, nicknamed 'squiggly' because of its S-shaped design. **Top Left**: the Glasgow Tower, part of the Science Centre complex and the tallest tower in Scotland. **Centre Left**: classic Glaswegian sandstone architecture. **Left**: Charles Rennie Mackintosh.

Tour 3

Merchant City

From Trongate's vibrant arts centres, this half-day ¾-mile (1.2km) walk delves into the heart of the Merchant City's cool hangouts, conversions and enterprising institutions

The Merchant City fell into decline during the 1980s recession, leaving huge warehouses abandoned and businesses boarded up. Ambitious developments and stylish conversions, added to visionary arts projects such as the Tron Theatre and Trongate 103, have brought the area back to life. Expect an earthy mix of arty creativity and working-class wit.

While other cities have wrestled with inner-city problems, Glasgow perversely had an outer-city problem. Huge schemes – Drumchapel, Easterhouse, Castlemilk and Pollok, which were created after World War II to facilitate slum clearance – stand guard at each corner of the boundaries. In the late 1970s and early 1980s, Glasgow was tagged

Highlights

- Tron Theatre
- Trongate 103
- Old Fruitmarket
- Ramshorn Kirk and Cemetery
- City Halls
- Old Glasgow Sheriff Court
- Hutchesons' Hall
- Italian Centre
- Trades Hall

Doughnut City – plenty round the outside and nothing in the middle. The Merchant City was Glasgow's attempt to bring life back to the central warehouse district. The square-mile area is now home to a core of

Left: the Glasgow Jazz Festival is held at the Old Fruitmarket *(see p.42)*.
Above: the stylish Trongate 103.

pavement. This is **Tron-St Mary's**, a former church. Like the street, it's named after the weighing machine, or tron, introduced by the Bishop of Glasgow in 1491 to weigh and tax goods coming into the city. The church has been operating as the **Tron Theatre** ❶ (tel: 0141-552 4267; www.tron.co.uk) since 1982, first as a club, and since 1990 as a full public venue. The Tron Theatre features a programme of both contemporary and traditional Scottish drama, and its restaurant – which offers cracking lunchtime and pre-theatre menus – is a popular meeting place.

Continuing westwards along the Trongate you come to the impressive **Trongate 103** ❷ (tel: 0141-276 8380; www.trongate103.com; Tue–Sat 10am–5pm, Sun noon–5pm), a massive Edwardian warehouse converted into an exciting arts centre, which opened in 2009. Beyond the cavernous contemporary atrium – imaginatively hewn out of the old handsome red-sandstone warehouse – are five floors of print studios, retail shops and galleries, where artists and the public can mingle and exchange ideas *(see box p.43)*.

young professionals and arty types. The blend of old and new architecture creates an exciting fusion which is echoed in the many restaurants serving up innovative cross-cultural food. Alongside exciting new arts developments including the Tron Theatre and Trongate 103 there's a wealth of pubs, clubs and independent shops. Keep your eyes peeled on partnership plans with Glasgow City Council for the Merchant City's next phase of arts-led regeneration, which is heading south of the Trongate, to create a cultural quarter down to the Clyde *(see p.39)*.

ALONG THE TRONGATE

Starting the route at the old heart of the city at **Mercat Cross** *(see p.14)*, go west along the Trongate. The tenements along each side date from the middle and end of the 19th century, and their rich facades funnel the street along to an almost Central European steeple whose base is an open arch across the busy

Above: exploring the Trongate, the old centre of the city.

UP ALBION STREET AND THE OLD FRUITMARKET

Crossing Trongate, head back east-wards then up Albion Street, past a magnificent red-sandstone bas-relief on the Cultural and Leisure Services building on the right, to the junction with Bell Street. This intersection has more pubs than the rest of both long streets put together. On the left, **Blackfriars** is large and lively, with a basement which hosts live music nights; **Café Gandolfi**, on the right, was one of the original Merchant City restaurants and contains the fantas-tical wood furniture of Tim Stead. **Gandolfi Fish**, an excellent seafood haunt, is just a few doors along. There are lots of lively pubs and restaurants which occupy various old buildings, including the **Old Fruitmarket ❸**.

The fruit market moved here from its former congested home in 1969 and now nestles, with the fish mar-ket, beside the M8 at Blochairn. The south end housed a successful general market for many years before clos-ing to accommodate the new pubs. The north end, however, lay closed

for years, until enthusiasts from the performing arts section of the council realised that its cobbled streets and balconied offices, which used to ring to the iron wheels of carts and the shouts of traders, would make an ideal, New Orleans-style venue for the annual

Above: Café Gandolfi has been serving for 25 years and is known for its good food and stylish interior.

Above: the Old Fruitmarket packs lots of period charm under its vaulted roof.

Glasgow Jazz Festival. The extensively refurbished Old Fruitmarket is a much-loved performance space and hosts regular events and parties.

The building above the excellent **Italian Kitchen** pizzeria and café, where Albion Street crosses Ingram Street, housed the original Mitchell Library collection on two floors in 1877. Stephen Mitchell came from a tobacco family and left a huge estate to provide books 'on all subjects not immoral' for the edification of the city's working classes. His initiative was the impetus

---

Ⓕ Scots and International Arts at Trongate 103

Resident organisations at Trongate 103 include the Russian Cultural Centre and Café Cosachock, Glasgow Print Studio, Street Level Photoworks, Transmission Gallery, Glasgow Project Room and Project Ability. Don't miss a journey into the darkly magic world of wonders and nuances of the Sharmanka (Russian for hurdy gurdy) Kinetic Theatre. This atmospheric space chimes with the workings of Edward Bersudsky and Tatyana Jakovskaya's fantastical inventions: a mesmerising, gently unfolding whirl of mechanical finds, *objets trouvés* and sculptural inventions, accompanied by crackly old Eastern European music.

Above: artworks for perusal at the Glasgow Print Studio.

Right: Ramshorn Cemetery is the final resting place of some illustrious figures.

for the public library service; today, the Mitchell Library (see p.63) is the largest public reference library in Europe.

On the opposite corner, Greenwich Village-style loft apartments are situated in a former Strathclyde University building. Further up Albion Street, the four-storey black-glass office formerly housed **The Herald** newspaper, which prides itself on being the world's oldest English-language daily. The newspaper has moved to offices in the city centre and the old offices have been turned into flats.

INGRAM STREET AND THE RAMSHORN

Looking right along Ingram Street, the **Ad Lib** bar/diner (tel: 0141-552 5736) on the right-hand side is housed in a red-sandstone building with a splendid coat of arms over the entrance. This was the Central Fire Station, built in 1899, and the home

of Wallace the Fire Dog, the mascot who faithfully escorted the engines on their dangerous missions. The engine room used to contain a memorial to the 19 firemen who died in the Cheapside Street whisky bond blaze in 1960, an event which still scars the memory of many families in the city.

As you turn left along Ingram Street, the **Ramshorn Kirk ❹** looms out of a grove of unlikely urban elms. The Gothic church with its square clock tower is properly known as St David's (Ramshorn) and was built in 1824 on the Ramshorn estate. Thomas Rickman, a Birmingham architect, was chosen to design the present building upon the site of an 18th-century 'God Box'-style church. Its alluring design is based on a late 13th- and 14th-century Gothic design. Those tall and narrow, beautifully proportioned dimensions, soaring stained-glass windows, and substantial crypt show all the hallmarks

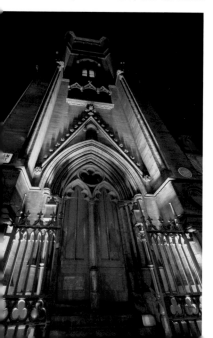

Left: lit up at night, the full impact of the Ramshorn Kirk's Gothic architecture can be felt.

Retail Therapy

The Merchant City has swanky boutiques and foodie places aplenty. **Boudiche** (203 Ingram Street; tel: 0845-475 0250) stocks chic lingerie labels including Stella McCartney and Christian Lacroix. If it's jewellery you're after, head to **Brazen** (8 Albion Street; tel: 0141-552 4551) where you'll find unique pieces by independent designers and cool watches by Lip. If your tummy is rumbling, go to **Peckham's** (61–65 Glassford Street; tel: 0141-553 0666), a superb deli with a fine selection of cheeses, wines, beers and gourmet treats downstairs, plus a sleek ground-floor café and a cooking school upstairs (see p.119).

Above: Peckham's sells delicious delicatessen goodies.

of Gothic Revival Scots Style. It is built in handsome blond sandstone mined from a nearby quarry at Cowcaddens, and its tower – towards the front of the building – is 120ft (36m) high and houses a set of bells which have never been rung. The building is now used by the Strathclyde University Theatre Group, which stages an eclectic repertoire in the small performance space (see local press for details) and uses the crypt as rehearsal rooms. The intimate, atmospheric space is well worth visiting, especially for a performance.

The **Ramshorn Cemetery** is a verdant respite from street noise and a fascinating voice from the past. Many gravestones are so old as to be illegible, and some are still barred and spiked against the predations of grave robbers. Emile L'Angelier, arsenic victim of the infamous Madeleine Smith, is buried here, as is David Dale, philanthropic co-founder of New Lanark, and John 'Phosphorus' Anderson, the ebullient father of Strathclyde University. On the pavement outside,

worn by thousands of careless feet, are the initials RF and AF, marking the resting place of the Foulis brothers, a pair of enterprising and painstaking printers who perfected the craft for Glasgow University in the 18th century. Robert Foulis was also instrumental in establishing an Academy of Arts some 14 years before the Royal Academy in London.

CITY HALLS AND CANDLERIGGS

The Ramshorn stands sentinel at the head of Candleriggs, a street which takes its name from the noisome candleworks which initially operated well away from the main population. This is the heart of the Merchant City, with coffee houses and fashionable bars on the right and the substantially refurbished **City Halls** ❺, where Dickens drew crowds for his readings and where every hue of political opinion has been heard, on the left. When the halls were built in 1841, they could accommodate an astonishing 3,500 people.

Above: the City Halls is a renowned concert venue.

The traditional shoebox-style auditorium is still renowned today throughout the world for its incredible acoustics. It's a busy hub for musicians which is well worth checking out: the Glasgow Centre for Music inside is a friendly organisation based here which has lots of information about upcoming concerts and public workshops. The BBC Scottish Symphony Orchestra is also based here; in addition, the auditorium hosts performances by the Scottish Chamber Orchestra. For all the latest about City Halls performances and affiliated venues nearby (the Old Fruitmarket, Glasgow Royal Concert Hall) pop in, call 0141-353 8080 or check out www.glasgowconcerthalls.com.

Further down on the left, the pavement outside the City Halls has some interesting marblework, created when the street cobbles were renewed and which reflects the area's age.

Below: Hutchesons' Hall has been at its present location on Ingram Street since 1806.

WILSON STREET

At the junction of Candleriggs and Bell Street, the **Glasgow Police Museum** (www.policemuseum.org.uk; summer Mon–Sat 10am–4.30pm, Sun noon–4.30pm, winter Tue and Sun, same hours; free) gives an insight into the history of Britain's first police force, as well as featuring exhibits on international policing.

Turning right from Candleriggs into Wilson Street, new flats mix with the imposing bulk of the old warehouse

The building is currently being used as the home of the Scottish Youth Theatre *(see box below)*, a retail complex and smart residential apartments.

Passing the **Brunswick Hotel** on the right, the flats at the corner of Brunswick Street and Ingram Street are a fine example of facade retention. The site was originally the warehouse premises of Campbell, Stewart & McDonald, and was one of the first in the Merchant City to tear out and replace the whole interior while keeping the architecturally important shell. The same thing is now happening with new district council buildings across the road.

district and smart design shops nestle below. Continuing right into Brunswick Street, a sandstone Victorian building with huge Ionic columns occupies the entire block. This was the **Old Glasgow Sheriff Court ❻**, which opened in 1892 and closed in 1984, having witnessed nearly a century of unmitigated villainy. It once housed a whipping table (now in Strathclyde Police's Black Museum in Pitt Street) and was said to be haunted by a lady in white.

HUTCHESONS' HALL

The white building on the opposite side of Ingram Street is **Hutchesons' Hall ❼**. Statues of George and Thomas Hutcheson, brothers from a landowning family, peer down from niches in the classical front.

On his death in 1639, Thomas Hutcheson made provision for a hospital for 12 'poore decrippet men'. George added more funds on his death two years later. The hospital was originally in the Trongate, and

---

⟨K⟩ Scottish Youth Theatre

Established in 1976, the Scottish Youth Theatre (Old Sheriff Court, 105 Brunswick Street; tel: 0141-552 3988; www.scottish youththeatre.org) organises an eclectic programme of classes and performances dedicated to young people of all ages, up to 25 years old. Productions are staged in the Brian Cox Studio (named after the Dundonian star of Hollywood blockbusters *Rob Roy*, *Braveheart* and *The Bourne Supremacy*) and theatres around the country.

Above: inside the light-filled Scottish Youth Theatre.

moved to its present location in 1806 to a design by David Hamilton, with further reconstruction work by John Baird in 1876. The interior is quite simply stunning. It was acquired in 1982 by the National Trust for Scotland (www.nts.org.uk) whose renovations over the years have been scrupulous and sympathetic. The building is, once again, undergoing restoration and is currently closed to the public.

ITALIAN CENTRE AND TRADES HALL

Just past Hutchesons' Hall is the pedestrianised concourse of the **Italian Centre 8** in John Street. In this short stretch, on a sunny summer day, Glasgow can consider itself to be a European city. White-aproned waiters rush back and forth to tables of animated diners talking on their

Below: the Italian Centre, with its restaurants and cafés, feels like a continental European city in summer.

mobiles below the restaurants' canopies. A bronze of Mercury keeps an eye on the shoppers with their Armani and Versace bags, and the view up through the arches of the City Chambers *(see p.51)* is a symphony in stone. Shona Kinloch's humorous sculpture entitled *Thinking of Bella* and the Zen-calm slow flow of a water feature counterpoise the clamour for *la moda italiana* fripperies.

Leaving the Italian Centre, the squat domed building on the corner of Glassford Street houses a retail outlet. The building was designed by John Burnet and is a splendid example of late Victorian confidence. Slightly further down on the same side is the **Trades Hall 9** (tel: 0141-552 2418; Mon–Fri 9am–4pm, Sat 9am–noon; self-guided audio tours available), which is, apart from the Cathedral, the oldest building in the city which still fulfils its original function. It is the home of the 14 trades of Glasgow, which include hammermen, fleshers, bonnetmakers, weavers and barbers (who were the early surgeons). Their symbol – 14 arrows bound together – adorns the magnificent curving staircase which leads into the grand hall. The hall is lined with a magnificent mirrored silk frieze – the 3-D of its time – showing the trades about their business.

The Trades Hall is also the home of the Trades House, whose business these days is mainly philanthropic – it dispenses more than £1 million a year in charity. It is worth a visit, especially for the benches carved by Belgian refugees in the entranceway, the Adam plasterwork and wood ceilings, and the kists, or chests, which are opened only once a year and contain a time capsule of trinkets dating back to 1604.

Return to Glasgow Cross by following Glassford Street south and turning right into Trongate.

Above: the Trades Hall offers a fascinating look at the 14 traditional city trades.

ⓔ Eating Out

Café Gandolfi
64 Albion Street; tel: 0141-552 6813; www.cafegandolfi.com; daily all day.
A stylish, light-filled bar-restaurant with beautiful wood furniture serving simply prepared dishes like linguine with crab, cherry tomatoes, coriander and chicken. Neighbouring Gandolfi Fish is its sleeker cousin. £

City Merchant
97–99 Candleriggs; tel: 0141-553 1577; www.citymerchant.co.uk; Mon–Sat lunch and dinner.
Quality modern Scottish cuisine specialising in meat and seafood. Try the superb Loch Etive oysters and mussels. ££

The Dhabba
44 Candleriggs; tel: 0141-553 1249; www.thedhabba.com; daily lunch and dinner.
Superb North Indian cooking; their speciality is dum pukht, curry cooked in a special dish that seals in the juices. Dishes such as tiger prawns from the clay tandoori oven are also recommended. ££

Ichiban Japanese Noodle Restaurant
50 Queen Street; tel: 0141-204 4200; www.ichiban.co.uk; Mon–Thur noon–10pm, Fri–Sat noon–11pm, Sun 1–10pm.
Minimalist, with steaming bowls of noodles served at long benches. £

Lily's
103 Ingram Street; tel: 0141-552 8788; Mon–Sat lunch only.
This great little café has veggie options and caters for kids. Alongside burgers and baked potatoes there are Eastern tastes including spicy chilli and vegetable Thai wraps. £

Rab Ha's
83 Hutcheson Street, Merchant City; tel: 0141-572 0400; www.rabhas.com; Thur–Sat dinner only.
This cosy restaurant offers seafood and meat classics. £

Tron Theatre Restaurant
63 Trongate; tel: 0141-552 8587; www.tron.co.uk; Sun–Mon lunch only, Tue–Sat lunch and dinner.
Serves no-nonsense British dishes using locally sourced ingredients. Great pre-theatre meal deals. £

Tour 4

City Centre

This 1-mile (1.6km) tour takes you from the sumptuous George Square and merchants' powerhouses to the shops of Buchanan Street, stopping to visit the Gallery of Modern Art

This half-day walk starts amid the bustle around Queen Street Station and the grand expanse of George Square, which contains the lavish City Chambers and the main tourist information office. Keep your wits about you amid the workaday melee as you will find your eyes are constantly drawn upwards to scan the wealth of mighty stonework built by Glasgow's old governmental and mercantile powerhouses.

Between visits to old bank building conversions and the experience of being swamped by the Buchanan Street shopping crowds, take a breather in the popular Gallery of Modern Art and enjoy the light-filled environs of one of the many swanky Princes Square top-floor eateries.

Highlights

- George Square
- City Chambers
- Glasgow Tourist Office
- Gallery of Modern Art (GoMA)
- Stock Exchange Building
- Buchanan Street and Princes Square Shopping
- Merchants' House

QUEEN STREET STATION AND CITY CHAMBERS

Queen Street Station, the starting point of this tour, runs frequent train services to Edinburgh, Dundee and all points north, as well as a suburban service from the Clyde coast to Lanarkshire. Built on the site of a witnessed momentous events in the square below, including the raising of the hammer and sickle by the Glasgow Soviet in 1919.

The interiors are a riot of marble, mosaic and alabaster. The vaulted ceiling of the entrance hall alone is covered with one and a half million Venetian mosaic tiles. Linger in the entrance hall, where tours begin and excited local schoolchildren often linger to admire the Chambers mosaic coat of arms on the floor, with arms that reflect legends about Glasgow's patron saint, St Mungo. There are four emblems: the bird, tree, bell and fish, as remembered in the following verse:

> *Here's the Bird that never flew*
> *Here's the Tree that never grew*
> *Here's the Bell that never rang*
> *Here's the Fish that never swam*

Left: Buchanan Street is always busy with shoppers. **Above:** George Square is a popular meeting place.

quarry in 1842 with a daring curved glass roof, it is Glasgow's oldest station. Beside it, **George Square ❶** began as a muddy hollow in 1781 and developed into a civic meeting place over two centuries. Its beautiful lawns have been replaced with red tarmac, much to the chagrin of office workers who used to sunbathe there at the first blink of sunshine.

The **Millennium Hotel** to the right of the station as you face it was, naturally, a railway hotel, and the BR initials can still be seen above the doorway.

The next office block on the left is best sped past in order to come to the **City Chambers ❷** (Ground Floor only, Mon–Fri 8.30am–5pm; guided tours of whole building, Mon–Fri 10.30am and 2.30pm; free), the towering statement of Glasgow's Victorian confidence, based on the east side of the square. It was opened in 1888 and, according to the architect, was a 'free treatment of the Italian Renaissance'. The ornate front has

F Glasgow Hotel Stories

It was at a Millennium Hotel (*see p.51*) dinner in 1941 that Roosevelt's World War II envoy Harry Hopkins pledged American support to Britain against Hitler with the biblical reply: 'Whither thou goest, I will go; and where thou lodgest, I will lodge; thy people shall be my people, and thy God my God.' Winston Churchill, who also had a Central Hotel suite during World War II, nearly choked on his cigar. A Glasgow myth goes that Roy Rogers also had a suite in those grand Central Station lodgings, and rode his horse Trigger up and down the main staircase.

Above: the American envoy – and eloquent speaker – Harry Hopkins.

Granite and marble staircases lead like Escher paintings to the council chambers where the Lord Provost (the Scottish equivalent of Mayor) presides over the city's affairs. There are seats for all 79 councillors, all facing the Lord Provost, his Depute, and the Chief Executive, who are seated behind the mace. If you are interested in visiting while the council is in session you can book a place in the public gallery which looks down on the proceedings, or take a pew in the small press gallery, from which much of the lively banter emanates during debate. Civic functions are regularly held in the great Banqueting Hall, under murals painted by 'Glasgow Boys' Henry, Lavery and Roche, which portray the city's colourful history.

Below: the Cenotaph in front of the City Chambers.

GLASGOW TOURIST OFFICE

Passing the white, lion-flanked monolith of the **Cenotaph**, the south side of the square begins with the former General Post Office, which has been redeveloped as offices and luxury flats. Across Hanover Street, the middle office on the block is that of the **Glasgow Tourist Office** ❸ (tel: 0141-204 4400; www.seeglasgow. com; May–June and Sept Mon–Sat 9am–7pm, Sun 10am–6pm, July–Aug Mon–Sat 9am–8pm, Sun 10am–6pm, Apr–Oct Mon–Sat 9am–6pm).

It's a grand space for learning all about the city, although queues to gain information can be very long and service can seem a tad slow. If you are

Above: the much-decorated statue of Wellington outside the GoMA.

leaflets and maps though, and to find information about travelling around all of Scotland. A small shop next to the information desk also sells specialist guide books, Ordnance Survey maps for outdoor enthusiasts and an entertaining selection of kitsch souvenirs.

GALLERY OF MODERN ART

Turning left down Queen Street, past bars and fast-food restaurants, the great pillared hall on the right in Royal Exchange Square is the **Gallery of Modern Art** ❹ (GoMA; tel: 0141-287 3050; www.glasgowlife.org.uk; Mon–Wed and Sat 10am–5pm, Thur 10am–8pm, Fri and Sun 11am–5pm; free). Guarded by a statue of Wellington by Baron Marocchetti (which revellers grace most Friday and Saturday nights with a traffic cone), the gallery was previously the Stirling Library. It grew out of a house owned by tobacco baron William Cunningham of Lainshaw, and the huge Corinthian columns at the front and the hall at the rear were added later.

really desperate, the tourist office can book accommodation on your behalf but it's not the best service and many leading hotels prefer to deal independently of VisitScotland, which gives you a clue as to the efficacy of the operation. It's a great place to pick up

Above: a striking view of the roof of the Gallery of Modern Art.

GoMA opened in 1996 to a welter of controversy about its collection. Many critics damned it for populism, but the citizens voted with their feet, and attendance continues to exceed expectations. It is divided into four galleries and there is a great café in the basement by the Martyr's Library. The cavernous ground-floor space retains its columns and original classical features, lending itself to bold pieces like Jim Lambie's eye-popping geometric floor of 2008, entitled *Forever Changes*. The upper galleries use natural light wonderfully, and concentrate on group shows which often tackle challenging themes.

In 2009, the exhibition *shOUT* caused a furore in the right-wing press and even stirred up condemnation from the Vatican. The show focused on gay, lesbian, transgender and intersex life – with explicit images created by the likes of Nan Goldin, David Hockney and Robert Mapplethorpe. One exhibit, *Made in God's Image*, in which visitors were invited to add comments to the pages of a Bible, attracted 600 complaints.

Above: St George's Tron on West George Street.

ST VINCENT PLACE

Returning up Queen Street and turning left, **St Vincent Place** ❺ opens up an august street of banks and offices faced with the full repertoire of Victorian masonry. The Clydesdale Bank on the north side has bas-reliefs, crouching men and encircled emblems

---

Ⓕ Handsome Pubs

Some of Glasgow's gorgeous, solid buildings are now devoted to the Glaswegian passion for having a blether over a drink. **The Counting House** (tel: 0141-225 0160) on the corner of George Square has been converted into a pub and restaurant with splendid interior statuary, cornicing and glass dome above the bar; **The Auctioneers** (tel: 0141-229 5851) in North Court is also a pub and restaurant furbished with the kind of bric-a-brac which used to pass through McTear's showrooms; and **78 St Vincent** (tel: 0141-248 7878) is beautifully lit by the vaulting windows of a former bank, and has an interior reminiscent of Le Chartier restaurant in Paris.

Above: the stunning interior of The Counting House pub.

Above: elegant buildings on St Vincent Place show off the Victorian stonemasonry that characterises much of the architecture in this district.

of the towns where the bank has had a presence. Opposite, the former Scottish Provident Building's red sandstone reaches skyward.

ST GEORGE'S TRON AND GLASGOW STOCK EXCHANGE

Passing a variety of city shops on the left, the tour turns right into West Nile Street and right again into West George Street. The church in the centre of the road is **St George's Tron** ❻, built in 1807 to accommodate the westward movement of the city. It was designed by William Stark, who was also responsible for a jail on Glasgow Green and a lunatic asylum. The Tron has a long tradition of being at the evangelical wing of the Church of Scotland: Tom Allan was a key figure in the Scottish evangelical movement of the mid-20th century, and if you pop in today you are sure to be greeted by an enthusiastic minister.

On the north side of the square, Nelson Mandela Place, is the former

Old Athenaeum which, on opening in 1888, offered classes in science, philosophy and literature to more than 1,000 students. It now houses shops and restaurants. Tucked into the corner is the Royal Faculty of Procurators Hall, with the heads of law lords carved on the window arches. On

Right: the red sandstone former Scottish Provident Building.

the other side of the square is the
early French Gothic extravagance
of the former **Glasgow Stock
Exchange ❼** building, which brings
to mind the London Law Courts and
is a rather rare flight of fancy amid
the solidity of its surroundings. It,
too, now houses shops.

BUCHANAN STREET

The wide avenue of **Buchanan
Street ❽**, the city's most prestigious
shopping arena, stretches southward.
It starts at Argyle Street, with Frasers
on its domed corner site, and leads
up a Victorian canyon fronted by
designer names. In the pedestrianised
centre is the winged *Spirit of St Kentigern* statue, and buskers, from lone
evangelists to full string quartets, provide daily entertainment.

Shopping

Further along on the right is the
Argyll Arcade, an enclosed walkway
lined with jewellers' shops, which right-
angles back to Argyle Street. Nearby is
the entrance to **Princes Square ❾**,
a beautiful mall packed with trendy
boutiques and bars on several levels.
It is best entered via the central escala-
tor, past the *trompe l'oeil* paintings of
worthies like Sir Thomas Lipton, Keir
Hardie and John Logie Baird.

On the top floor, while looking
down at the mosaic of the central
well, you will not fail to notice the huge
Foucault's Pendulum, a replica of
the device by which Jean-Bernard-
Léon Foucault proved the rotation
of the Earth in the dome of the Pan-
theon in Paris in 1851. The centre is a

BUCHANAN STREET
CITY CENTRE

Above: the ornate Glasgow Stock Exchange building.

veritable shopaholic's dream, with the presence of top names in fashion such as Vivienne Westwood, as well as upmarket high-street chains like Ted Baker, while the top floor has a range of cafés, bars and restaurants including the stylish Darcy's, Barca Tapas and Cava Bar, November and Cranachan.

It's a wonderful building to visit and especially welcome during a rainy spell of Glasgow weather – not uncommon of course – as the twinkly lights, inviting shops and top-floor cafés provide a cheery diversion before braving the elements again.

Galleries and
Royal Concert Hall

Back on Buchanan Street, the shopping choice is wide, from chic labels and brands like Hugo Boss, L'Occitane and Apple. Weary shoppers can stop at the Mackintosh **Willow Tea Rooms** *(see Eating Out p.99)*, which is a replica based on the many remnants of the architect's original restaurant

Left and Below: out and about on Buchanan Street.

Above: the Willow Tea Rooms *(see pp.57 & 99)* re-create the designs by Charles Rennie Mackintosh for a restaurant at the turn of the century.

designs owned by the City Council, or **Rogano** ❿, a splendid Art Deco shellfish restaurant in the passageway leading to Royal Exchange Square.

Past Graham Tiso, Hobbs and The White Company and back across St Vincent Street to the Stock Exchange, the view northwards takes in the

Buchanan Galleries, an enormous shopping complex development which encompasses several city blocks and a pedestrianised area at the **Glasgow Royal Concert Hall** ⓫ (tel: 0141-353 8000; www.glasgowconcerthalls.com), the main venue for classical concerts. The centrepiece here is a statue of the late Donald Dewar, credited as the driving force behind the new Scottish Parliament.

MERCHANTS' HOUSE

Returning along West George Street to George Square, the oriel-windowed **Merchants' House** ⓬ (tel: 0141-221 8272; Mon–Thur 9am–12.30pm, subject to functions) reflects the confidence and self-importance of the guilds which created it. Housing the Chamber of Commerce, which is the second-oldest in the world after that of New York, it hosts occasional concerts (see local press for details).

The original Merchants' Hall, constructed around 1600, acted as a

Left: Rogano is an Art Deco *tour de force* and a memorably decadent dining experience.

meeting place for merchants and as an almshouse for merchants and their families who had fallen on hard times. The Hall was rebuilt in the 1650s to a design by Sir William Bruce of Kinross, who would later be architect to King Charles II. The old layout consisted of ground-floor lodgings for old couples and facilities for pensioners. The imposing present-day building was opened in 1877 according to a design by John Burnet; his son added two storeys in 1908. The Merchants' House of Glasgow bought part of the estate of Wester Craigs in 1650, and funded the landscaping of the city's grand Necropolis in the 1830s (see p.22).

Above: the dome of the Merchants' House is topped by a sailing ship.

E Eating Out

Barca
Level 2, Princes Square; tel: 0141-248 6555; daily noon–midnight.
Wonderful traditional Spanish tapas such as prawns in chilli sauce and chorizo sausage or a full paella of meat or fish (two people sharing), as well as a cava bar just for drinks. £

Bread and Butter
74 Buchanan Street; tel: 0141-221 4383; www.breadandbutterglasgow. co.uk; daily lunch (Sat until 6pm).
Located down a side alley, this café-bar with a club downstairs serves up great-value British grub including hearty pies. £

Darcy's
The Courtyard, Princes Square; tel: 0845-166 6012; Mon–Sat lunch and dinner, Sun lunch only.
For some café-style panache in the Princes Square shopping centre, book a red-leather booth at this basement joint. As well as decent coffee, the varied menu includes Scots Angus burgers and Thai green chilli. ££

Rogano
11 Exchange Place; tel: 0141-248 4055; www.roganoglasgow.com; daily lunch and dinner.

Glasgow's homage to the days of ocean liners and cocktails exudes 1930s glamour. Top-class service and the place for oysters. Dress up. £££

Sloans
62 Argyll Arcade, 108 Argyle Street; tel: 0141-221 8886; www.sloans glasgow.com; daily lunch and dinner.
An Edwardian-style pub-restaurant with Grade A-listed interiors including a grand ballroom and a cosy, snug bar. Serves simple British cuisine. £

The Social
27 Royal Exchange Square; tel: 0845-166 6016; daily lunch and dinner.
A swanky bar full of suits by day and dressed-up Glaswegians by night with a brasserie menu that includes pasta dishes, juicy steaks and veggie-friendly wraps. There is also a decent brunch menu at weekends. £

Urban Bar & Brasserie
23–25 St Vincent Place; tel: 0141-248 5636; www.urbanbrasserie.co.uk; daily lunch and dinner.
This stylish bar-restaurant, housed in the former Bank of England HQ, has a monthly brasserie menu with excellent fish and meat creations. Perennial favourite is the fish soup. ££

Tour 5

Going West

This 1¼-mile (2km) walk follows architecturally fascinating St Vincent Street to the historic Mitchell Library, then on to the cutting-edge CCA arts centre – all in half a day

The city has been moving west since medieval times, and, since the more prosperous were the first to decamp, the buildings become noticeably more ornate. Starting the route at the junction of Hope Street and St Vincent Street, the Victorian offices spiral upwards in ever more detailed flights of the stonemason's fancy. Looking south, the clock tower of the Central Hotel looms above Central Station, the main link to the south, in an austere welcome.

UP AND DOWN ST VINCENT STREET

St Vincent Street, named after the naval battle at Cabo de São Vicente, is a thoroughfare devoted to Mammon, so it is fitting that its long incline is

Highlights

• St Vincent Street Free Church of Scotland

• The King's Theatre

• Mitchell Library

• Tenement House

• CCA: Centre for Contemporary Arts

crowned with one of Scotland's finest temples to God. On the way up the hill, there's a beguiling mix of imposing classical, Art Nouveau, Art Deco and modernist buildings including: the old **Phoenix Assurance building** (1913) in American Classical style at No. 78, the eccentric **Hatrack** (1902) with its rich red sandstone, stained glass and spiky lead roof at No. 142–144, and the elegant 1929-built Royal **Sun Alliance Building** at No. 200, with its angular Art Deco statue added in the 1930s.

St Vincent Street Free Church of Scotland ❶ is the best remaining example of the work of Alexander 'Greek' Thomson (1817–75). Thomson, paradoxically, is famous for being Glasgow's 'forgotten architect', forever in the shadow of Charles Rennie Mackintosh (see p.97). Like Mackintosh, he wanted to design every detail of a commission, down to the decorations on the walls. This is the only one of his three city churches still intact, and it has been added to the World Monument Watch for endangered buildings. Light from enormous windows bathes the sumptuous interior, and a recently repaired tower, which recalls India rather than Greece, dominates Blythswood Hill.

On the right, slightly further down the hill, the needle spire of **St Columba's Gaelic Church** soars heavenwards. It has its roots in the influx of

Left: steep St Vincent Street. **Above**: Alexander Thomson's St Vincent Street Free Church of Scotland.

Highlanders who flocked to the city in the 18th and 19th centuries after the Clearances, when landlords evicted crofters to make way for sheep.

The western end of St Vincent Street is enveloped by the roar of the traffic on the M8, which cuts through an underpass on its way to Edinburgh. The marble and mirrored glass tower on the left is the **Hilton International ❷**, a once state-of-the-art hotel (built in 1990) which is looking a bit tired inside and out these days.

TOWARDS MITCHELL LIBRARY

Turning right into Elmbank Street, the white building on the right is the former **High School**, with statues of Galileo, Cicero, Homer and James Watt. The school dates back to the 15th century, but it has gradually moved west from its original home and is now situated in more space in Anniesland. Today, the buildings are occupied by council offices. On the corner of Elmbank Crescent, the ornate grey-stone building provides rehearsal rooms for Scottish Opera and Scottish Ballet, two of Scotland's most prestigious companies. It used to be the home of the Institute of Shipbuilders and Engineers, and a bronze plaque just inside the entrance pays tribute to the engineers who went down at their posts on the *Titanic* in 1912.

The King's Theatre ❸ (tel: 0844-871 7648), on the corner of Elmbank Street and Bath Street, was the most fashionable Glasgow venue of the Edwardian age. Built in 1904, with a lion mascot in stone above the entrance, it provides a stage for a variety of shows, catering for most ages and tastes. Expect lots of West End-style musicals – such as *Chicago* and *Blood Brothers* – stand-up comedy shows from the likes of Frankie Boyle and Dave Gorman, and the odd ballet production or popular musical extravaganza chucked in for good measure. The **Griffin Bar** opposite the theatre dates from the same period. Known as The King's Arms up until 1969, the refurbished (2008) Griffin is a 'B' listed building with original wooden interiors, window panels and lead work. It's worth popping your head in and ordering a pint and a sneaky

Below: the Mitchell Library is the largest of its kind in Europe.

Childhood Life in the Auld Tenements

A tour around the 1892-built Tenement House (see p.64) makes for a thought-provoking and fun visit for adults and kids alike. It's not often you can hear the tick-tock of the grandfather clock while poring over old labels and utensils around the basic kitchen range. Eyes and minds wander through the assorted contents – old jam jars, food tins and household bills – and back in time to a much simpler cramped existence.

Above: the Tenement House reveals Glaswegian life in years gone by.

wee dram to take a closer gander at the main bar, with its handsome tiled floor and back-to-back rows of fixed leather seats.

Mitchell Library

Heading left down Bath Street through a canyon of modern offices, the splendid dome of the **Mitchell Library** ❹ (www.glasgowlife.org.uk; Mon–Thur 9am–8pm, Fri–Sat 9am–5pm, closed Sun), adorned with its statue of Minerva, rises above the motorway traffic. It was the legacy of tobacco heir Stephen Mitchell, and, after homes in Ingram Street and Miller Street, the collection moved to the present site in 1911. It is now the biggest public reference library in Europe, and its comprehensive Glasgow Room is a boon and a blessing to those with an interest in the city. Take a peek inside and the friendly janitor will direct you along the handsome marble and darkwood lined corridors. There's a good little café next to the modern IT suite amid miles of crazy, lurid geometric carpet and books.

The Mitchell Library has fabulous, free resources for those looking to research family history or anyone just curious about the city's past. Level 3 and the Family History Section is

manned by knowledgeable staff who help people from all over the world delve into records such as the Glasgow newspaper archive (starting in 1715), censuses, war deaths, parish registers and monumental inscriptions. Leaf through the trade directories to discover intriguing old professionals like the phrenologist who studied the skull's lumps and bumps to determine personality traits.

Below: the ornate King's Theatre stages a wide range of productions.

Above: the red sandstone grandeur of Charing Cross Mansions.

BACK EAST TO TENEMENT HOUSE

Up North Street past the excellent **Black Sparrow** pub *(see Eating Out, opposite)* and across Sauchiehall Street, the ornate fountain at Charing Cross may not have the cachet of Pisa, but the drunken angle at which it leans is every bit as dramatic. Walking north, head for the pedestrian bridge which spans the motorway. A

Below: the CCA is known for staging an eclectic programme.

pause here affords a close-up look at the graceful red-sandstone curve of Charing Cross Mansions and, on the left, the turrets, arched windows and balconies of St George's Mansions, both testament to the graciousness into which tenement living evolved.

It pays to keep this Edwardian splendour in mind on the walk from the end of the bridge on the path up through grass and trees to the **Tenement House ⑤** (www.nts.org.uk; Mar–Oct daily 1–5pm, last admissions 4.30pm; charge). It lies at the end of the walkway at 145 Buccleuch Street and is fascinating because it offers a glimpse of tenement life. It was the home for 50 years of a spinster who changed nothing in her 'wally close' (tiled common stairway). The gaslit parlour, black range and rosewood piano are, as the National Trust for Scotland which now runs it says, 'a sure sign of gentility'.

Returning along Buccleuch Street, turn right into Garnet Street and then left into Hill Street: this was for many years the heart of the ethnic Chinese community. On the other side, Italy is recalled by the domed grandeur of **St Aloysius Church**, which is attached to the Jesuit school further up the street.

Above: Charing Cross Mansions detail.

CCA – CENTRE FOR CONTEMPORARY ARTS

Turn left down Scott Street to hit Sauchiehall Street, renowned for its vibrant nightlife, music venues and bars. At No. 350 stands the superb **Centre for Contemporary Arts** ❻ (CCA; tel: 0141-352 4900; www.cca-glasgow. com; gallery Mon–Sat 10am–6pm; free), which has six exhibitions a year and mounts an eclectic programme. Alongside the changing visual arts exhibitions there are interactive performance-based art workshops, cinema screenings (lots of independent films, shorts, documentaries and classics) and a superb programme of musical events, ranging from improvised soundscapes to traditional Gaelic nights and dancey DJ sets. Visiting performers and artists from all over the world mean you never know what strange delights might be on the bill. The glass-roofed courtyard café is a wonderful space and the Saramago Café Bar has a stylish terrace with some of Glasgow's best weekend music events.

⒠ Eating Out

Black Sparrow
241 North Street; tel: 0141-221 5530; www.theblacksparrow.co.uk; daily noon–9pm.
Stylish bar with decent food menu that includes mains such as mustard-crusted salmon and pork belly in cider batter. Also serves up a selection of burgers and pizzas. £

CCA Café
30 Sauchiehall Street; tel: 0141-352 4920; Mon–Sat 10am–10pm.
A vegetarian venue offering a variety of mezze dishes, salads and mains such as courgette and lemon linguine, served in a wonderfully airy enclosed courtyard. £

The Living Room
150 St Vincent Street; tel: 0141-229 0607; daily lunch and dinner.
Cocktail-style glitz, popular with an after-work crowd. Live music is played on the baby grand piano most evenings. ££

Loon Fung
417 Sauchiehall Street; tel: 0141-332 1240; daily lunch and dinner.
Long-established but still admirable Cantonese cuisine, much frequented by the Chinese community. £

Malmaison Brasserie
Malmaison Hotel, 273 West George Street; tel: 0141-572 1000; daily lunch and dinner.
The restaurant in this smart hotel chain serves brasserie classics with high-end presentation. The grill offers a variety of steaks as well as lobster and there's curry made with Scottish mutton. £

Mussel Inn
157 Hope Street; tel: 0843-289 2283; www.mussel-inn.com; daily lunch and dinner.
Features the best of west coast seafood – oysters, scallops, prawns and, of course, mussels. ££

Two Fat Ladies
118a Blythswood Street; tel: 0141-847 0088; www.twofatladiesrestaurant.com; daily lunch and dinner.
An elegant dining room – usually packed – serving seafood creations such as seared scallops, sea bream and ling, plus enticing desserts. ££

D.I.Y. Glasgow

Glasgow's music and arts scenes have a D.I.Y. spirit at their heart and, for many, the city's rough-hewn edge makes a refreshing change from London, Paris, New York and Venice

The flux of Glasgow's riverside post-industrial landscape – all old decrepit warehouses rubbing alongside sleek, contemporary architecture – seems to flow into the city's creative population. Likewise its indie music labels eschew the corporate and bland, creating a vibrant scene with lots of great bands and venues.

AN ART LEGACY

The swinging doors of the Charles Rennie Mackintosh-designed **Glasgow School of Art** (GSA) building continue to whir with the comings and goings of students and artists. It was the home

of the influential *fin-de-siècle* Glasgow Group of modern artists – which included Charles Rennie Mackintosh – and also boasts celebrated alumni such as Alisdair Gray, Ian Hamilton Finlay, and contemporary artists Jim Lambie, Roddy Buchanan and Simon Starling.

Glasgow's D.I.Y. spirit flourished in the late 1970s and early 1980s, when the city was deep in recession and blighted by sectarian violence. New Glasgow Boys and Girls took over warehouse spaces and set up gallery collectives, the most influential being **Transmission** in 1983 (www.trans

continues. The GSA is building a new teaching and research centre. Studio collectives are renovating warehouses and government-led partnerships continue to regenerate the Merchant City by creating a cultural quarter.

A THRIVING MUSIC SCENE

Glasgow's music scene was born out of bedroom obsession with exotic sounds. In 1979, the D.I.Y. punk ethos of Postcard Records squeezed Orange Juice and Edwyn Collins from bedroom to Top of the Pops. The city's Gaelic roots, flirtation with Country and popular Americana can be heard in the uplifting Motown beats and West Coast jangly pop of many Glasgow bands. Teenage Fan Club recast the sunshine harmonies of the Byrds and Big Star in late 1980s Glasgow. Some have an art-school sensibility, like Franz Ferdinand, while Electronica DJ duo Slam mined Teutonic beats and Detroit techno music, founding Soma Quality Recordings in 1991.

A good place to start is the independent record shop-café-venue **Monorail** (www.monocafebar.com), part owned by Pastels front man Stephen McRobbie. It stages film nights, gigs and other cultural events, including the odd appearance by artist David Shrigley.

missiongallery.org). By 1996 contemporary art was part of the mainstream and Glasgow got itself a grand building to showcase its artists: the **Gallery of Modern Art (GoMA)**. Arts hubs **CCA** (Centre for Contemporary Arts), **Tramway** and **Trongate 103** followed.

Both the **Glasgow Art Fair** and **Glasgow International Festival** – the city's answer to the Venice Biennale – attract an international crowd. The impetus

Alongside big venues like the **Scottish Exhibition and Conference Centre** (SECC; *see p.10*), there are many intimate venues and bars where Glasvegas, The Fratellis and Camera Obscura regularly appear. Top names include the legendary **Barrowland Ballroom** (www.glasgow-barrowland.com/ballroom). **O2ABC** (www.o2abcglasgow.com) and **King Tut's Wah Wah Hut** (www.kingtuts.co.uk) host established indie bands. **Nice N' Sleazy** (www.nicensleazy.com) and **Stereo** (www.stereocafebar.com) showcase up-and-coming acts. **Òran Mór** and **Captain's Rest** on the Great Western Road, West End, are also on the music map.

Above: a work by Jim Lambie at GoMA. **Top Left**: the band Glasvegas at Nice N' Sleazy. **Centre Left**: a work by David Shrigley. **Left**: the Glasgow School of Art is key to this scene.

Tour 6

From Kelvingrove to the Clyde

This half-day, 2.5-mile (4km) stroll around the green surroundings of Kelvingrove Art Gallery and Museum leads to museums and landmarks on the Clyde waterfront

This walk is a welcome escape from the noisy M8 and is a journey to the heart of Glasgow's Victorian achievements as part of the British Empire. Calm prevails along curving streets lined with handsome Victorian sandstone terraced houses, and the twisting paths around leafy Kelvingrove Park lead to the impressive Kelvingrove Art Gallery and Museum. Then it's all modern achievement with the new architectural highlights of 21st-century Glasgow.

Highlights

- Lobey Dosser
- Kelvingrove Park
- Kelvingrove Art Gallery and Museum
- Riverside Museum
- Glasgow Science Centre

Left: an exhibit at the Kelvingrove Art Gallery and Museum. **Above:** the beloved statue of Lobey Dosser.

LOBEY DOSSER AND PARK CIRCUS

Glasgow is peppered with bronze memorials commemorating the cream of Queen Victoria's empire, but the statue that holds the fondest place in the hearts of Glaswegians is of a mustachioed sheriff astride a two-legged horse. It is to be found at the start of this walk on the corner of Woodlands Road, which runs west from Charing Cross and Park Drive.

Lobey Dosser ❶, as the statue is called, was the creation of newspaper

Ⓢ West End Shopping

The West End has an interesting array of independent shops, most of which are just north and west of this route on Byres Road and Great Western Road. Among the foodie places near the start of this walk is **Grassroots Organic** (20 Woodlands Road; tel: 0141-353 3278; Mon–Wed 8am–6pm, Thur–Fri 8am–7pm, Sat 9am–6pm, Sun 11am–5pm), an organic wholefood market with lots of healthy takeaway options including pasta dishes, burritos and salads. **Damselfly Crafts** at 380 Great Western Road (tel: 0141-341 0119; Mon–Sat 9.30am–5.30pm, Sun noon–5pm) is a colourful craft shop with lots of gift ideas. Nearby **Galletly & Tubbs** (431 Great Western Road; tel: 0141-357 1001; Mon–Sat 9.30am–5.30pm, Sun noon–5pm) stocks elegant home furnishings and artworks.

Above: Grassroots Organic sells a selection of tasty wholefood treats.

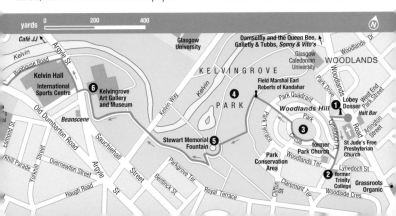

cartoonist Bud Neill who, more than anyone before or since, captured the city's sharp but skewed sense of humour. Regulars in the **Halt Bar** across the road were instrumental in raising the public subscription in 1992 to the memory of the Sheriff of Calton Creek and his masked adversary Rank Bajin. The question 'What was the name of Lobey Dosser's horse?' has sparked a thousand pub arguments, and knowing the answer (El Fideldo) will give you instant credibility with Glaswegians.

Leaving the mix of antiques shops and restaurants in Woodlands Road, the route runs from the spire of St Jude's Free Presbyterian Church up through the greenery of Woodlands Hill and left into Lynedoch Place. This wide street leads to an area of flats and offices dominated by the Italianate towers of **Trinity College ❷**, formerly the college of the Free Church and now converted into much sought-

Above: a statue of a scholar on a bridge over the River Kelvin.

after flats. Along with the lonely white tower of the Park Parish Church – the rest of it was demolished in the late 1960s – they form a dramatic focus for the city skyline.

Above: autumn colours in Kelvingrove Park.

Ⓖ Cycling and Walking along the Kelvin Walkway

There are lots of fabulous opportunities for cycling and walking in and around Kelvingrove Park and the Botanic Gardens. One less well-known route follows the Kelvin Walkway and links up with the Forth and Clyde Canal towpath at the Kelvin Aqueduct – an impressive feat of 18th-century engineering and architecture, which was once the largest functioning aqueduct in Europe. Ask at the tourist office in George Square for detailed maps and consult the Ordnance Survey Explorer map 342.

Above: a handy marker denotes the Kelvin Walkway.

Turn right into Park Circus Place and enter the splendid oval of **Park Circus ❸**, with its air of Victorian elegance. The grand curving terraces rising to a bluff above the River Kelvin were designed as private housing for the emergent middle classes by Charles Wilson (1810–63) and can justly be regarded as his masterpiece.

KELVINGROVE PARK

They lead to **Kelvingrove Park ❹**, the first custom-built park in the city and site of three great International Exhibitions, in 1888, 1901 and 1911, which proudly proclaimed Glasgow's contribution to the British Empire.

The Victorians viewed public parks as the lungs of their smoky cities, allowing their workers the physically and morally beneficial effects of clean air and uplifting scenery. **Glasgow Green** (see p.31) was the only public space in the city until 1846, when a grand plan was proposed by the city council to create three huge sculpted parklands – **Kelvingrove** in the west, **Alexandra Park** in the east and **Queen's Park** (see p.87) in the south – under the hand of designer Sir Joseph Paxton, of Crystal Palace

fame. The city now boasts more than 70 parks, and although the recreations reflect Victorian tastes – boating ponds, playgrounds, putting and bowling – the work of the inventive and industrious Parks Department has given each its own character.

Above: a Trinity College tower in the Park district.

The entrance to Kelvingrove Park is guarded by a spectacular statue of Field Marshal Earl Roberts of Kandahar (1832–1914), surrounded by the bas-relief trappings of his Indian campaigns. There is a similar statue of the field marshal in Calcutta. The park itself is a fine example of the ornamental pleasure garden, with winding paths and wide boulevards. Descending into the park, the main thoroughfare and bridge are marked by a memorial to the officers and men of the Highland Light Infantry who fell in the 'South African War' or Boer War (1899–1902). Turning left here, the road leads through dappled shade to the extravagance of the **Stewart Memorial Fountain ❺**, a tribute to the Lord Provost who, in 1855, finally managed to secure a supply of pure water to the city from Loch Katrine in the Trossachs.

Turning right past the skateboard park and the duck ponds, the tour

Above: in the Kelvingrove Art Gallery and Museum.

emerges onto the Kelvin Way, and a bridge cornered by four groups of bronzes representing peace and war, commerce and industry, shipping and navigation, and prosperity and progress. They were badly damaged by German bombers in 1941 and restored by sculptor Benno Schotz 10 years later.

KELVINGROVE ART GALLERY

The path opposite the park gate leads to the red-sandstone grandeur of **Kelvingrove Art Gallery and Museum ❻** (tel: 0141-276 9599; www.glasgowlife.org.uk; Mon–Thur and Sat 10am–5pm, Fri and Sun 11am–5pm; free), a superb repository of one of the finest civic collections in Europe. The gallery had its origins in the paintings of Trades House Deacon Convenor Archibald McLellan, which the city acquired in 1854 along with his gallery in Sauchiehall Street. The need to house these and other displays led to the 1888 Exhibition – a mammoth event attended by Queen Victoria and nearly 6 million of her subjects – and the profits were used as pump-priming money for the new building. The project was conceived on a breathtaking scale, with

Below: the Stewart Memorial Fountain in Kelvingrove Park.

Above: some say that the Gallery was built the 'wrong way round', because the main entrance is from Kelvingrove Park, while most visitors enter from Argyle Street.

its twin towers, which shelter a massive bronze of St Mungo, facing the lacework spire of Glasgow University, and the other side leading down a grand staircase onto sunken gardens. Visited by over 1 million people each year, the Kelvingrove reopened its impressive interior in 2007 after a £27.9 million, three-year refurbishment. Its enormous galleries are arranged around two naturally lit halls on either side of the Great Hall, which has an immense Lewis pipe organ still used for recitals.

Kelvingrove's Art Collections

The collection, which includes more than 8,000 objects over three floors and many interactive displays, also

◖ Discovery Centres and New Enlightenment

The Kelvingrove Art Gallery and Museum also has much to appeal to children. Glaswegian kids and visitors wander around excitedly and open-jawed, taking in myriad exhibitions, lifelike scale models of animals and the Spitfire LA68 (City of Glasgow Squadron), hanging from the ceiling of the west court. As well as the child-friendly exhibits there are Discovery Centres (info: 0141-276 9505) dedicated to art, environment and history, while the Centre of New Enlightenment (TCoNE; info: 0141-276 9506), in the Campbell Hunter Education Wing, offers interactive educational adventures for young people aged 10 to 14 years.

Above: the Spitfire LA68 is suspended above the west court.

Above: Kelvin Hall now houses a major sports centre.

features many 17th-century Dutch, French Impressionist and post-Impressionist paintings. Rembrandt's *Man in Armour*, Millet's *Going to Work* and Dalí's *Christ of St John of the Cross* are particular favourites. The Glasgow School, in the forefront of the departure from classical tradition, and the Scottish Colourists are well represented, and among the 3,000 oils and 12,500 drawings and prints are works by Rubens, Pissarro, Van Gogh, Degas, Matisse and Monet. Within the walls of this cultural treasure trove, visitors to the West Wing will find a World War II Spitfire hanging from the ceiling *(see box p.73)* and Sir Roger, a stuffed elephant that was once a resident of Glasgow Zoo.

Leaving from the west end of the art gallery, past the 'machine-gun Tommy' war memorial, cross the street to the **Kelvin Hall** (tel: 0141-276 1450), which for many years was Glasgow's foremost exhibition centre, fondly remembered for its annual carnival and circus, complete with elephants and their distinctive aroma. Built in 1927, it served for 60 years – including war service as a barrage balloon factory – before its functions were transferred to the Scottish Exhibition and Conference Centre next to the Clyde. It is now known as the **International Sports Centre** (Mon–Tue and Thur 7.15am–10pm, Wed 10am–10pm, Sat 9am–5pm, Sun 9am–8pm), which includes an athletics track, a climbing wall and a gym, and stages occasional events such as wrestling and basketball.

RIVERSIDE MUSEUM AND THE TALL SHIP

From Argyle Street turn left down Bunhouse Road and then right on to Old Dumbarton Road. Continue to the end of the road, under the railway bridge and take the underpass beneath the Expressway to reach the impressive sight of the **Riverside Museum** ❼ (tel: 0141-287 2720; www.glasgowlife.org.uk; Mon–Thur and Sat 10am–5pm, Fri and Sun 11am–5pm; free). This striking new multi-million-pound transport museum, designed by Zaha Hadid, opened in 2011 and has quickly become one of the UK's top ten attractions. More than 3,000 objects trace the history of transport, most of them relating to Scotland, from a velodrome of bicycles suspended from the ceiling to a wall of classic cars spanning the decades. Most popular, particularly with children, are the old trams, bus and subway carriage – climb aboard to get a real sense of travel in days gone by. Continuing the nostalgic theme, there are two areas recreating streetscapes

Above: the Riverside Museum at Pointhouse Quay was developed for the Museum of Transport. It opened in 2011.

from the 1890s to the 1960s with replicas of specialist shops and pubs.

To the rear of the museum is **The Tall Ship ❽** (tel: 0141-357 3699; www.thetallship.com; daily Mar–Oct 10am–5pm, Nov–Feb 10am–4pm; charge). The restored *Glenlee*, a Clyde-built three-masted barque, sailed the globe from the 1890s to the 1920s – the boat made journeys as far afield as Japan, Argentina and Australia – before becoming a naval training ship. The four decks can now be explored to find out what life was like on board. Visit the crews' cabins, galley, hospital and map room.

Next to The Tall Ship, **Seaforce** (tel: 0141-221 1070) runs exciting powerboat rides along the Clyde, weather permitting.

ALONG THE CLYDE

Return to the front of the Riverside Museum and follow Stobcross Road, running parallel with the busy Pointhouse Road, around to the SECC and the Clyde Auditorium. Unless you're attending a conference or a concert at the **Scottish Exhibition and Conference Centre (SECC)** (tel:

0844-395 4000) or the neighbouring **Clyde Auditorium ❾** (tel: 0141-248 3000) you're unlikely to go inside either of these two colossal buildings. But the architectural splendour – particularly of the latter, known affectionately as the 'Armadillo' – makes them must-sees and they have become symbolic of the whole regeneration of Glasgow from the 1980s onwards. The acclaimed architect Sir Norman Foster took inspiration from this former ship-building area, designing an exterior intended to emulate ships' hulls. On a sunny day, as the light hits the silvery curves, it's a stunning sight. Adjacent to these two buildings, yet

Above: the Finnieston Crane is no longer in active use, but remains as a landmark to Glasgow's industrial heritage.

another live venue, The Hydro, is currently under construction and due to be completed in 2013.

Walking down towards the river along Lancefield Quay, the hulking **Finnieston Crane** comes into view. This huge cantilever crane was in use for more than 50 years as a means of lifting heavy machinery, but it became redundant as industry died out in the city in the 1990s. Today, however, it stands as a dramatic tribute to the great industrial heritage of Glasgow.

ACROSS TO PACIFIC QUAY

At Congress Road on the riverfront take the footbridge over the Clyde, looking to your left as you do so to admire the Clyde Arc Bridge, also known as Squinty Bridge to the locals and another great symbol of modern Glasgow.

Turn right onto Pacific Drive then follow the signs to the **Glasgow Science Centre ❿** (tel: 0141-420 5000; www.gsc.org.uk; Wed–Fri 10am–3-pm, Sat–Sun 10am–5pm; charge). The main permanent attraction here is the planetarium, with various dif-

ferent staged exhibits to demonstrate and explain the solar system and the universe by exploring the night skies, but the science halls, with plenty of interactive exhibits for adults and children alike, hold great appeal too.

Above: the Glasgow Tower is the tallest tower in Scotland.

Above: the Science Mall and the IMAX theatre - two of the buildings that make up Glasgow Science Centre.

An IMAX theatre is also on site, while further along the quay and associated with the science centre is the rotating **Glasgow Tower**, a 416ft (127m) freestanding edifice. In theory, visitors can ride to the top via a lift for 360 degree views of the city. However, the tower has been plagued by engineering problems since opening, so don't be too disappointed if it's out of operation.

To return to the city centre, backtrack to the SECC and take bus No. 100 to George Square.

Eating Out

For the best eating options, see the adjoining Tour 7's Eating Out box, p.85. There's a great café in the Kelvingrove Art Gallery. Other options include these deli-cafés and an Oriental restaurant near the SECC:

Beanscene
1365 Argyle Street; tel: 0141-357 4340; daily breakfast, lunch and dinner.
There are three of these outlets in the West End offering a relaxed setting where you can pick from the varied blackboard menu, which usually offers tempting cakes, tapas, nachos, pizza and rice dishes. £

Café JJ
180 Dumbarton Road; tel: 0141-357 1881; daily lunch and dinner.

A homespun place with a selection of vegetarian enchiladas, pasta dishes, panini, crêpes and cakes. £

Sonny & Vito's
52 Park Road; tel: 0141-357 0640; daily lunch only.
A popular and friendly deli just off this tour, which serves excellent home-made sandwiches, pies, tarts, salads and sweet treats including huge apricot and chocolate muffins. £

Yen
28 Tunnel Street; tel: 0141-847 0330; daily lunch and dinner.
In a lovely rotunda building next to the SECC, Yen specialises in cuisine from the Far East: Japanese teppan-yaki dishes on the ground floor; classic Chinese and Thai dishes on the first floor. £–££

Tour 7

West End

Explore the West End's enthralling academic collections, boho Byres Road and the luxuriant Botanic Gardens on this 1.3-mile (2km) tour, which will take a minimum of 4 hours

In the hungry 1930s, the young bucks of Govan would cross on the Kelvinhaugh Ferry on a Sunday afternoon and stage their own version of the Latin *paseo* (walking out) with the local girls along the bosky grandeur of the Kelvin Way. And to the boys from the shipyard tenements it must have seemed like a foreign country. This wonderful walk takes in the Kelvin Way – which cuts through Kelvingrove Park – to the fascinating Hunterian art and museum collections on University Avenue, before exploring the boho shops, cafés and restaurants of Byres Road and Ashton Lane. Our jaunt continues to the exotic hothouses of the Botanic Gardens and ends amid Glasgow artist Alasdair Gray's vibrant murals at the Òran Mór cultural centre.

Highlights

- Kelvin Way
- Wellington Church
- Glasgow University
- Hunterian Museum
- Hunterian Gallery
- Byres Road
- Ashton and Cresswell Lanes
- Botanic Gardens
- Òran Mór

KELVIN WAY AND GLASGOW UNIVERSITY

Starting at the Sauchiehall Street end of the **Kelvin Way**, the Art Galleries open up on the left and the imposing Gothic front of Glasgow University

Left: winter walkers cross a snowy bridge over the River Kelvin.

looms on Gilmorehill. Mature trees canopy the Way after it crosses the bridge with its four dramatic bronzes by Paul R. Montford. On the right is the Kelvingrove bandstand, now sadly derelict (although a restoration is planned), and by an azalea-studded rockery further along on the left sit statues of the figures of the great scientist Lord Kelvin (1824–1907) and surgery pioneer Joseph Lister (1827–1912), both in their university robes.

At the end is a cluster of university buildings, with the imposing gothic

Glasgow University Union straight ahead and the Gilmorehill Centre in a former church on the right. Turning left onto the hill of University Avenue is the gilded gatehouse of **Pearce Lodge ❶**, a remnant of the 17th-century Old College in the city centre, which until recently housed the very 21st-century Computing Service.

Uphill on the right is **Wellington Church ❷**, a grand classical structure influenced by the Madeleine in Paris, with 10 massive fluted pillars supporting its portico. Its predecessor stood in Wellington Street in the centre of the city and attracted a well-to-do congregation, evidenced by the fact that its war memorial lists mainly officers, with only a scatter of enlisted men. There is a small café in the crypt. Next door is the bright, galleried circle of **The Reading Room ❸**, a quirky but practical study area built in the grounds of Hillhead House, given to the university in 1917 in memory of city merchant Walter MacLellan of Rhu.

Glasgow University ❹, directly across from the Reading Room, is one of the world's great seats of learning, with an outstanding academic history (*see p.15*) and worldwide influence. The University of Glasgow is the fourth oldest in Britain after St Andrew's, Oxford and Cambridge. In 1870 it moved to its current site, a leaded-windowed building designed by Sir John Gilbert Scott in what he called 'a 13th or 14th century secular style… with Scottish features'. A complex wrought-iron gate carrying the motto *Via Veritas Vita* contains the names of

Above: Glasgow University is one of the most prestigious in the country.

such luminaries as Bute, Kelvin, Lister, Watt, Stair, Adam Smith and Foulis.

HUNTERIAN MUSEUM

Just inside the gate is a monument to William and John Hunter, the medical brothers whose collection forms

Above: inside the fascinating Hunterian Museum.

Lord Kelvin's Inventions

The Hunterian Museum's displays dedicated to Lord Kelvin are a big hit with children. There are lots of hands-on activities, scientific instruments, demonstrations and digital images that bring the work of the Victorian scientist to life. Memorable displays include listening to music from a flame, seeing Kelvin's name lit by high-voltage electricity and testing your capacity to be a human battery.

Above: imaginative interactive exhibits at the Hunterian Museum.

the basis of the newly refurbished Hunterian Museum, and the award-winning **Visitor Centre** ❺ (Mon–Sat 9.30am–5pm) provides comprehensive information with guided tours of the university (May–Sept Wed–Fri and Sat 11am and 2pm, Oct–Apr Wed 2pm; charge).

A staircase by the Visitor Centre leads to the sunlit quadrangles and the contrastingly gloomy cloisters. Here also is the lusciously ornate Bute Hall and the **Hunterian Museum** ❻ (www.gla.ac.uk; Tue–Sat 10am–5pm, Sun 11am–4pm; free), Scotland's oldest, which displays the death mask of founder William Hunter. Its splendid galleries house material of great antiquity, from dinosaurs' eggs and rare material from Captain Cook's voyages to ancient coins and a history of the Romans in Scotland. Leaving by the Visitor Centre and turning left, you reach The Square, home to the Principal's residence and the University Chapel.

HUNTERIAN GALLERY

Directly across from the university gatehouse is the refurbished **Hunterian Gallery** ❼ (Tue–Sat 10am–5pm, Sun 11am–4pm; free) and the Mackintosh House within (see p.97), with its internationally famous Whistler collection and works by

Rembrandt, Pissarro, Sisley and Rodin. The museum has put together an impressive collection of contemporary art in recent years through the National Collecting Scheme for Scotland. All the recently acquired works have a naturalistic, scientific element that complements the overall collection. The fascinating work of Mark Dion is

Above: there is a rich collection of Old Masters at the Hunterian Gallery.

Above: Mackintosh's *Porlock Weir* at the Hunterian Gallery.

inspired by the powerful historic role of great museum collections such as the Hunterian's. Other contemporary art highlights worth seeking out are Christine Borland's delicate skulls entitled *Family Conversation Piece: Head of Father* (1998), and Matt Collishaw's strutting peacock, which accompanies the works of Whistler.

Above: the Ubiquitous Chip restaurant (*see Eating Out p.85*) is a mainstay of Ashton Lane.

The University Library, which contains more than 2.5 million books and journals, is just a few steps further up Hillhead Street.

BYRES ROAD

Abandoning academia for more hedonistic pleasures, **Byres Road**, at the junction with University Avenue, presents itself as the students' playground. Named after a small *clachan*, or village, which once stood there called Byres of Partick, it is a cosmopolitan mix of restaurants, bars and cafés, and comfortingly solid tenement architecture. Kember and Jones (No. 134), an upmarket deli and café, and The University Café (No. 87) are both excellent eateries on Byres Road. A brief detour up Highburgh Road opposite the junction leads to **Cottiers** ❽ (tel: 0141-357 5825), a superb theatre, bar and restaurant in a Victorian Gothic church by architect William Leiper, featuring the beautifully restored stained glass and interior design of Daniel Cottier. It hosts shows by Scottish Opera and Scottish Ballet, as well as experimental companies. Jazz is played on Sundays, 5–8pm.

This leads down an alley into an explosion of constantly busy bars and restaurants. In less than 100 yds/m, this narrow, cobbled lane offers Brel (tel: 0141-342 4966), with Belgian beer and 'rustic' food, Cul de Sac (tel: 0141-334 4749), an eclectic bar and restaurant, the Grosvenor Cinema with its huge loft café-bar (tel: 0845-166 6028), Jinty McGuinty's packed Irish bar, the Ubiquitous Chip *(see Eating Out p.85)* and the Ashoka Indian restaurant (tel: 0141-337 1115). Ruthven Lane close by has antiquarian bookstores and vintage and designer clothes.

CRESSWELL LANE

Going north up Byres Road past Hillhead Underground and Curlers, an old coaching inn, turn right into Great George Street and then left into **Cresswell Lane** for De Courcy's Arcade, a warren of stalls selling linen, jewels, games and records. At the end, turn left and then right again

Above: Ashton Lane is a focus for eating out and nightlife.

ASHTON LANE

To return to the route, just before University Avenue reaches Byres Road, turn right into Ashton Road and right again into **Ashton Lane**.

Ⓢ Shopping Frenzy

Independent boutiques and foodie outlets line Byres Road, while Ruthven Lane and De Courcy's Arcade in Cresswell Lane lure vintage fashion and 20th-century antiques fans. Vintage store **Circa Vintage** (37 Ruthven Lane; tel: 0141-334 6660) bursts with interesting threads, jewellery and curios. At No. 382 Byres Road, **Demijohn** (tel: 0141-337 3600) is a self-styled 'liquid deli' full of whiskies, liquors, oils and vinegars. The sweet-toothed will head for **I Love Candy** (261 Byres Road; tel: 0141-337 3399), filled with tempting old-school sweets, lollipops and Scots fudge. Still on Byres Road, at No. 388, **Boxwood** (tel: 0141-357 6642) features rustic home furnishings, twee treats and quirky clothes. Bookworms will enjoy

a visit to **Voltaire & Rousseau** (12–14 Otago Lane; tel: 0141-339 1811), a wonderfully dusty second-hand bookshop, crammed full of finds and collectable first editions.

Above: sweet treats galore at I Love Candy.

Above: inside one of the Kibble Palace glasshouses, at the Botanic Gardens.

into Byres Road to the junction with Great Western Road. On the right is the pyramid spire of the former Kelvinside Parish Church, which has been converted into the Òran Mór music centre, restaurant and bar. On the left is the terrace of the **Hilton Grosvenor Hotel**, a quarter-mile repetition of the facades of Venetian palaces. The eastern half was destroyed in a fire in 1978 and rebuilt with glass-reinforced concrete cast from the original pillars.

Directly opposite are the city's **Botanic Gardens** ⓫ (Gardens: daily 7am–dusk, Glasshouses: 10am–6pm,

Above: Òran Mór is a cultural centre in a converted church.

winter until 4.15pm, Visitor Centre: 11am–4pm; free), a restful recreation garden relocated from Sauchiehall Street to Kelvinside in 1842, with a herb garden, vegetable garden (highlighting a number of uncommon species) and walks along the Kelvin. The dramatic glasshouses nurture tropical plants. The delicate dome of the Kibble Palace was brought here from the Clyde coast home of John Kibble in 1873. An impressive structure, covering 23,000 sq ft (2,137 sq m), it was originally designed by John Kibble for his home at Coulport on Loch Long in the 1860s, and the components were cast by Walter Macfarlane at his Saracen Foundry in Possilpark.

Prime Ministers Benjamin Disraeli and William Gladstone were both installed as rectors of the University of Glasgow under the curved wrought-iron roof in the 1870s – these were the last public events to be staged here before the palace became solely used to house temperate plants. After a £7 million restoration, which involved its complete dismantling and the repair of its rusty parts, the palace was reopened in 2006. The ruins of the Botanic Gardens railway station – opened in 1896 and closed in 1939 – can be seen at the side of the gardens through railings.

Just up Queen Margaret Drive on the right is a building that once housed the women students of Queen Margaret College, as well as the old BBC headquarters, which is due to be converted into a luxury hotel.

ÒRAN MÓR

Just across from the Botanic Gardens on the city-bound section of the Great Western Road is the fine old Kelvinside Parish Church, converted and opened in 2004 as **Òran Mór** ⑫ (meaning 'great melody of life' or 'big song'). This cultural centre offers bars, venues and an eclectic programme of musical and theatrical events (including the afternoon A Play, A Pie and A Pint series). Pop

Above: studying the plants in the Botanic Gardens.

in to view the cavernous auditorium and its wonderful murals by artist and novelist Alasdair Gray.

Return to the city centre by bus from Great Western Road or by Underground from Hillhead (Byres Road) or Kelvinbridge (down Great Western Road).

E Eating Out

Balbir's
7 Church Street, West End; tel: 0141-339 7711; www.balbirsrestaurants.co.uk; daily dinner only.
Don't let the soulless interior fool you. This is an excellent choice for a quick curry packed with flavour and fresh ingredients. £–££

Little Italy
205 Byres Road; tel: 0141-339 6287; www.littleitalyglasgow.com; daily lunch and dinner.
This popular Italian does takeaways and eat-in pizzas, pasta dishes and delicious Portuguese custard tarts. ££

Naked Soup
6 Kersland Street; tel: 0141-334 8999; daily lunch only.
This small wood-panelled eatery is the place to find hearty, delicious casseroles, curries and soups such as tomato with mascarpone and chickpeas. £

No. Sixteen
16 Byres Road; tel: 0141-339 2544; www.number16.co.uk; daily lunch and dinner.
No. Sixteen serves impressive cuts of fish and meat, including sea bream

and braised belly of pork, with imaginative accompaniments. ££

Stravaigin
28 Gibson Street, Hillhead; tel: 0141-334 2665; www.stravaigin.com; Mon–Thur dinner only, Fri–Sun lunch and dinner.
Renowned for serving up the finest local ingredients with a laid-back vibe. Standouts include chargrilled Aberdeen Angus steak, mussels with chilli and coriander, and root vegetable Wellington with mushroom velouté. ££

Ubiquitous Chip
12 Ashton Lane; tel: 0141-334 5007; www.ubiquitouschip.co.uk; daily lunch and dinner.
The Chip is an institution in a converted mews stable. Enjoy fresh Scottish ingredients and a wonderful wine list amid stylish surroundings and playful artworks by Alasdair Gray. £££

The Wee Curry Shop
29 Ashton Lane; tel: 0141-357 5280; Mon–Sat lunch and dinner, Sun dinner only.
Mother India's chain of curry shops offers a vast array of spicy offerings at reasonable prices. £

Tour 8

South Side

Heading south of the Clyde, this 8-mile, half-day tour takes in parks, grand old houses and arty attractions aplenty, from the Tramway to the Burrell Collection

This tour travels amid abandoned factories and red-bricked chimney stacks, the landmarks of Southside's post-industrial past. First stop is the old Copelawhill Tram Shed reborn as Tramway, a contemporary arts centre renowned for its fabulous visual and performance art shows, and its magical Hidden Gardens. Nearby Queen's Park offers magnificent views towards Loch Lomond and Lanark, while heading west, the wide green expanse of the Pollok Estate contains woodland walks, opportunities for mountain biking, and the late 18th-century period grandeur of Pollok House.

The famous Burrell Collection, containing priceless artworks, is displayed in stunning, light-filled galleries close by. There are more uplifting delights at

Rouken Glen and the walled, verdant oasis at Greenbank Garden, with its elegant Georgian mansion built by an 18th-century tobacco merchant. If you don't have the use of a bike, a car would be the best means of transport for this tour, since it is not feasible on foot and public transport is complicated.

Queen's Park Views

Queen's Park rises to an impressive summit, with panoramic views as far as Ben Lomond in the north and Lanark in the south. Near the main walkway is an oak tree planted by Belgian refugees after World War I and a beech tree planted in 1945 to commemorate the 20th anniversary of the founding of the United Nations.

Left: the sweeping view from Queen's Park over Glasgow and its glorious backdrop of hills.

HEADING SOUTH TO TRAMWAY

Start this walk from Argyle Street at Jamaica Street and, crossing Glasgow Bridge – built in 1899 following a Thomas Telford design – get in the middle lane, pass the classical tenements of **Carlton Place** to the left and head south along Eglinton Street. This area was a riverside hinterland for much of the 20th century and still bears the marks of commerce with warehouses, disused factories and railway arches.

On Albert Drive, the road leading to Pollockshields East railway station, is the fabulous **Tramway ❶** arts centre (tel: 0845-330 3501; www.tramway.org; Tue–Fri noon–5pm, Sat–Sun noon–6pm; free) below a red-brick chimney stack. It is known for its compelling programme of visual and performance art, dance and experimental music. The Scottish Ballet is now based at Tramway too, in superb new studio facilities.

The majority of the art shows explore challenging, adult-orientated themes which may not be suitable for children. This shouldn't dissuade families from visiting the centre, though, as one of Tramway's most popular attractions is its urban sanctuary, the Hidden Gardens, which sprouted from factory wasteland. Audioguides are available to help you identify the birdsong while you are walking around. Tramway's café-bar has views of the garden and is a great place to refuel and relax.

QUEEN'S PARK

Head east via Coplaw Street across to parallel Victoria Road, a wide avenue of small shops, pubs and restaurants which leads to the gates of **Queen's Park ❷**. Although built in the reign of Victoria, and laid out by Sir Joseph Paxton of Crystal Palace fame, these rolling grounds take their name from Mary, Queen of Scots, whose supporters lost the Battle of Langside nearby in 1568. The 148-acre (60-hectare) park

Above: Pollok House mounts an impressive collection of Spanish art, in addition to works by William Blake.

occupies a commanding site, which was considerably enlarged in 1894 by the enclosure of the grounds of Camphill. It is a wonderful place for a picnic and has lots of amenities, should you be feeling more active, including five floodlit tennis courts, pitch and putt,

bowling greens and a skateboard park. There is also a pond teeming with birdlife, including tufted ducks, moorhens, mallards, little grebe, coots and mute swans. The large boating pond provides serene moments during the summer months.

TOWARDS POLLOK HOUSE AND COUNTRY PARK

Turning left at the gates, Langside Road, which is not signposted, runs round the park past the **Victoria Infirmary** – a huge hospital serving the whole of the south side of Glasgow – to the monument on Battle Place, designed by Alexander Skirving in 1887, and an imposing stone-cleaned former church which has been converted to the Church on the Hill bar and restaurant.

Going straight ahead at the roundabout, follow Millbrae Road into Langside Drive, turn right at Newlands

Left: a snowy day brings out the sledges in Queen's Park.

Above: light streams into the bucolic Pollok Country Park.

Road (you'll see a sign for Diarsie House School) and follow it to Riverford Road. Go through the Pollokshaws area, once a thriving working-class heartland but now much demolished to make way for modern housing and a new railway line, and turn right onto Barrhead Road for the entrance to the Pollok Estate.

These beautifully sculpted grounds were given to the city as late as 1966 by Mrs Anne Maxwell Macdonald and now form **Pollok Country Park ❸**, where morning joggers and evening strollers enjoy the Highland cattle, heavy horses, art collections and woodland walks. The driveway runs past the Police Dog and Mounted Branch and parkland grazed by 'toffee-wrapper' cattle with their glowering fringes to **Pollok House ❹** (tel: 0844-493 2202; www.nts.org.uk; daily 10am–5pm; charge), a masterful William Adam construction dating from 1752. Its exquisite interior retains many original features and houses a fine collection of Spanish School paintings, and the gardens – including a particularly fine parterre and a full and productive walled garden – are bounded by a lazy curve of White Cart Water.

It has undergone a sympathetic restoration programme, and there is a good café-bar in the kitchen. Pollok Country Park offers wonderful surroundings for cycling and is reached via Routes 7 and 75 of the National Cycle Network (www.sustrans.org.uk), or take your bicycle to Pollokshaws West station from Glasgow Central.

Ⓖ Cycling and Mountain Biking

Pollok Country Park has three mountain-bike circuits suitable for different abilities. The **Green Circuit** offers a gentle ride; the **Blue Circuit** has steeper, more varied terrain and requires more skill; the **Red Circuit** is more akin to wild mountain topography and is not for the faint-hearted. Those seeking more two-wheeled thrills should head a few miles further south to **Cathkin Braes Country Park**, which is the venue of the Commonwealth Games 2014 Mountain Biking event.

Above: Pollok Country Park is ideal for cyclists of all abilities.

Above: Sir William Burrell's incredible collection of artefacts from all over the world is on display at the famed Burrell Collection.

Above: medieval archways have been incorporated into the Burrell Collection's building.

BURRELL COLLECTION

Retracing the tour and forking left leads to the internationally famous **Burrell Collection** ❺ (tel: 0141-287 2550; Mon–Thur and Sat 10am–5pm, Fri and Sun 11am–5pm; free), the outstanding legacy of the shipping magnate Sir William Burrell, whose collector's instinct and eye for a bargain were on a par with his occasional rival, the American newspaper magnate William Randolph Hearst. He perfected the business method of selling his fleets of ships in a boom period and buying in a slump, and realised his considerable fortune in 1916 when he sold up to concentrate on his first love, art.

The collection is eclectic and idiosyncratic, with more than 9,000 objects from Egypt, Greece, the Middle East and South and East Asia, plus tapestries and stained glass from medieval Europe. Favourites with Glasgow visitors are the Degas collection, Rodin's *Thinker* (one of 14 casts made from the original) and the *Warwick Vase*, an 8-ton marble which dominates the courtyard. Volunteer guides with specialist knowledge lead tours of the Burrell Collection – for a detailed list of upcoming tours tel: 0141-287 2550 or consult the website www.glasgow life.org.uk.

In Glasgow City Council hands

Glasgow city received this fascinating collection in 1944 in a bequest of restrictive conditions, largely concerning Burrell's fears about the potential damage to his treasures from industrial air pollution. This meant that they lay in storage until 1983 when cleaner air and the acquisition of Pollok Estate allowed the construction of an award-winning building with deceptively simple lines, which has drawn as much admiration as the museum's contents.

Medieval archways from the collection are blended with new red sandstone, and some halls have glass walls to the floor, giving the impression that the exhibits are being viewed in the open air. Others are completely enclosed and provide a warmly lit backdrop for some of the world's most exquisite tapestries. The collection also includes exhibits of entire rooms from Burrell's home at Hutton Castle in Berwickshire, and there's an excellent café-restaurant.

Above: the imposing *Warwick Vase* is the centrepiece of the Burrell Collection's courtyard.

ROUKEN GLEN PARK

The road out of the park on the left – look for the carved woodpecker – leads onto Haggs Road. Turn right, get in the middle lane and follow it to Pollokshaws Road and the Round Toll roundabout, then take the B769 for Thornliebank. Stay on this road until the next roundabout and turn

Family Tours

The Burrell Collection organises special tours for kids and families that explore art, crafts and scientific themes. Perennial favourites include the Weaving Magic tour, which has a hands-on workshop, the Charcoal Fun drawing class with an artist, and Hidden Treasure, which challenges children to solve clues and find the booty, always a popular activity! For the latest events tel: 0141-287 2564.

Above: the collection offers several absorbing child-friendly activities.

Above: a sculptural feature in the Greenbank Garden.

left onto the A727 for East Kilbride. Soon after joining the dual carriageway, take a right turn into Rouken Glen Park.

Rouken Glen Park ❻ was donated to the city by Mr A. Cameron Corbett (later Lord Rowallan) in 1906 and passed to the adjoining Eastwood Council in 1984, after a dispute over running costs. Its loss to Glasgow was felt on an emotional level by many who remembered school trips to the large boating pond, where a motor launch would carry day-trippers round the islands, much to the indignation of nesting ducks.

Fears of the park's demise, however, were groundless, and a thriving range of commercial concerns – an attractive garden centre, art gallery and a signposted walkabout trail – have given it a new lease of life. The old attractions, however, remain unchanged: the waterfall tumbling into a mossy glen, the walled garden, a golf course and generous parkland.

Below: Rouken Glen's natural waterfall was doubled in height in the early 1800s.

GREENBANK GARDEN

Turning right at the exit, follow the A727 over Eastwood Toll roundabout, through the suburbs of Clarkston to Clarkston Toll, where Greenbank Garden is signposted on the first right after the roundabout.

Greenbank Garden ❼ (garden: daily 9.30am–sunset; shop and tearoom: Nov–Mar Sat–Sun 1–4pm, Apr–Oct daily 11am–5pm; house: Apr–Oct Sun 2–4pm; charge), which lies on Flenders Road, off Mearns Road, is a substantial walled garden which many city dwellers regard as an oasis of calm. It is one of the few substantial properties the National Trust for Scotland has near the city. The gardens surround a tobacco merchant's 18th-century mansion; there are tours of the interior with its remarkable billiard room most Sunday afternoons. A tennis court has been converted into a garden for disabled visitors, with raised plant beds; the floral profusion encourages wildlife.

To return to the city, go to Clarkston Toll and follow the signs for the M77, taking junction 3 for the city centre.

Above: the atmospheric walled Greenbank Garden is set around an 18th-century house.

🅴 Eating Out

Boaters Café
Rouken Glen Park; tel: 0141-638 3078; daily, closed evenings.
This homely café located on the edge of Rouken Glen Park is very popular with families who queue for the ice cream. Savoury options include panini, salads, pasta dishes and fish and chips. £

The Kitchen Restaurant
Pollok House, Pollok Estate, 2060 Pollokshaws Road; tel: 0844-493 2202; daily lunch only.
Amid the grand basement interiors of this award-winning restaurant, discerning diners are served a limited but excellent choice of mains including good veggie options. The home-baked cakes are legendary. £

Moyra Jane's
20 Kildrostan Street; tel: 0141-423 5628; Tue–Sat lunch and dinner, Sun–Mon lunch only.
This former bank building has marble-topped tables and wood-panelled walls – suitably solid surroundings for traditional, quality fare including lamb dishes, Thai fishcakes, vegetarian moussaka and massive meringues. £

Tramway Café-Bar
25 Albert Drive; tel: 0845-330 3501; Jan–Oct Tue–Sat 9.30am–8pm and Sun noon–6pm, Oct–Dec Tue–Sat 10am–6pm and Sun noon–6pm.
An airy space looking onto the Hidden Gardens serving excellent, healthy vegetarian and pasta dishes, superb lamb burgers and sandwiches. £

Tour 9

Mackintosh Tour

Charles Rennie Mackintosh, pioneer of the Modern Movement, left the city of Glasgow a handsome artistic and architectural legacy which never ceases to inspire

Rarely has a whole industry been founded on the designs of one architect, but Charles Rennie Mackintosh (1868–1928) was no ordinary architect. His vision and originality were at the forefront of the Modern Movement, and his imaginative buildings and clean, simple interior design were unique. Many of Mackintosh's buildings, however, were sadly neglected until the 1980s, but then his importance was realised and much-needed restoration of his works commenced. They lie spread across the city and a comprehensive day tour moving from one gem to another is difficult, but the following guide highlights the most accessible and representative works, which are marked with an ⓜ on the maps.

Highlights

- The Lighthouse
- Glasgow School of Art
- The Mackintosh House
- Queen's Cross Church
- The Hill House
- House for an Art Lover
- Scotland Street School
- The Willow Tea Rooms

The best source for information about Mackintosh himself, the history of the buildings and about access to Mackintosh properties as well as specialist tours is the **Charles Rennie Mackintosh Society** (tel: 0141-946 6600; www.crmsociety.com). They

Left: the House for an Art Lover (p.98) is based on Mackintosh's drawings.

have an ongoing campaign to increase awareness of the architect and a push to have Mackintosh buildings designated as Unesco World Heritage sites. The **Glasgow Tourist Information Centre** (see p.123) is another valuable port of call. It's worthwhile buying a one-day Mackintosh Trail Ticket

(£16) which allows visitors entry to all participating Mackintosh attractions and unlimited travel on the SPT subway and First bus services.

CITY-CENTRE SIGHTS

Starting in the city centre, **The Lighthouse** (tel: 0141-276 5360; www.glasgow.gov.uk; tours Mon, Wed–Fri 10.30am–5pm, Tue and Sat 11am and 3pm; charge, Sat free) features a

Above: an architectural exhibit at The Lighthouse.

Mackintosh Interpretation Centre to place the artist in his cultural context and help visitors find his buildings. Built to a Mariscal design beside the tower of the old *Glasgow Herald* building in Mitchell Street, its rooftop platform offers close-up views of his work. It hosts a variety of temporary exhibitions exploring design and architectural themes and has a fabulous café. In 2009, the Lighthouse Trust organisation – set up to champion Scottish architecture and design – found itself in financial trouble and went into administration. However Glasgow City Council stepped in to keep the centre open and there are now plans afoot to extend it further into a National Centre for Architecture and Design.

GLASGOW SCHOOL OF ART

Along Sauchiehall Street and up Scott Street on the right is Mackintosh's crowning achievement, the **Glasgow School of Art** (www.gsa.ac.uk; guided tours Apr–Sept daily 11am–5pm on the hour, Oct–Mar Mon–Sat 11am and 2pm; charge for tour). One of the most venerable art schools in the UK,

every stone, window and railing is redolent of the architect's unique style.

The east wing was started in 1897 under the influence of revered headmaster Fra Newbery, but the west wing was not completed until 1909. Hefty sandstone block and soaring gridded oriel windows make the first glance of 'the Mac' as you approach from a steep hill laden with drama. Inside there are dark, woody spaces with handsome detailing – the church-

Above: the Queen's Cross Church houses the Mackintosh Society HQ.

Above: the Glasgow School of Art.

like library with its grid-layout wooden pillars and hanging lights is one of the many inspiring spaces Mackintosh created. Studios and windowsills in far-flung corners are bathed in light and provide awesome views. A visit to the building – join one of the guided tours with an expert if you can – gives a compelling insight into this working building which continues to inspire art students more than 100 years after its inception.

MACKINTOSH IN THE WEST END

In 1906, Mackintosh completely redesigned the interior of an ordinary terraced house at 78 Southpark Avenue for himself and his wife Margaret, whom he had married in 1900 just before being made a full partner at Honeyman & Keppie. They lived in it for eight years and, before it was demolished in 1963, the fittings were removed and are now on display as the **Mackintosh House** (charge) in the **Hunterian Gallery** (see p.81; Tue–Sat 10am–5pm, Sun 11am–4pm), which is a brief taxi ride from the School of Art.

Another short taxi hop away from here is the **Queen's Cross Church** in Garscube Road, which is now the headquarters of the **Charles Rennie Mackintosh Society** and is open to visitors. After admiring the red-sandstone exterior with its unusual blocky turrets, dip your head inside to marvel at the interiors. The blue stained-glass window designs play on the Gothic style to startling effect, while the handsome relief carving on wood and stonework complements the feeling of sparseness, light and space. As well as being the best place for finding out

Ⓕ Rennie Mac's Early Years

One of 13 children of a police superintendent, he was born in Parsons Street, where he would later create the Martyrs' School. He attended night classes at Glasgow's School of Art – then in the McLellan Galleries – before joining Honeyman & Keppie, for whom he did his best work. His first major public building, the former *Glasgow Herald* office – renamed The Lighthouse in a design by Barcelona Olympics maestro Javier Mariscal – was the focal point of Glasgow's year as City of Architecture in 1999.

Above: Glasgow's architectural hero, Charles Rennie Mackintosh.

Above: the House for an Art Lover, set in attractive gardens.

about Mackintosh events and tours, the Mackintosh Church at Queen's Cross has a superb library. The shop stocks an extensive range of Mackintosh books and objects based on the great man's designs.

THE HILL HOUSE AT HELENSBURGH

The Hill House (tel: 0844-493 2208; Apr–Oct 1.30–5.30pm; charge) is not in Glasgow, but it should be included in any tour of Mackintosh works. A 40-minute train ride away in Helensburgh (First Scotrail; tel: 0845-748 4950), it's by far the most attractive of his domestic commissions. Built on a commanding site for the publisher Walter Blackie, the fittings have been meticulously conserved by the National Trust for Scotland.

SOUTHSIDE MASTERPIECES

House for an Art Lover (www.houseforanartlover.co.uk; Apr–Sept Mon–Wed 10am–4pm, Thur–Sun 10am–1pm, Oct–Mar Sat–Sun 10am–1pm; tel: 0141-353 4770; charge) was created from a portfolio which Mackintosh presented for a design competition in 1901. Following his drawings, the house was built in a beautiful parkland setting beside the Victorian walled garden in Bellahouston Park, and contains striking details and interiors, plus a café and shop. The nearest underground station is Ibrox; nearest mainline station is Dumbreck. The house is about 15 minutes by taxi from the city centre.

Scotland Street School (tel: 0141-287 0500; www.glasgowlife.org. uk; Tue–Thur and Sat 10am–5pm, Fri and Sun 11am–5pm; free) is most easily reached by underground. Get off at Shields Road station, and the school's twin towers of leaded glass and red sandstone are clearly visible across the road.

Built between 1903 and 1906, the school is clearly Glasgow-style and offers a fascinating look at developments in Scottish education. There are interactive displays which explore the school world and design tools to see if you can match the master draughtsman Mackintosh. Even more fascinating are the accounts of former pupils' recollections of their school days. The archive follows the decades, detailing the minutiae of childhood and background events in Scottish and world

Above: inside the elegant House for an Art Lover.

history. Themes covered include classroom discipline, school trips, school attire, evacuation and World War II, playground antics and the changing local environment. The excellent Back to School role-playing programme has interactive displays allowing the visitor to experience the classes of yesteryear (see box opposite).

Ⓔ Eating Out

Art Lovers Café
House for an Art Lover, Bellahouston Park; tel: 0141-353 4770; daily lunch only.
Set within one of Mackintosh's finest houses, this popular café is open to people visiting the house and those who simply want to come and eat. The elegant surroundings embody Mackintosh's design ideals, and the dishes are presented with style and skill. The menu places huge emphasis on seasonal produce so it changes regularly, but you may find sea bass, Aberdeen beef or pork belly at any given time. In summer there is a lovely outdoor seating area. £

The Willow Tea Rooms
97 Buchanan Street; tel: 0141-204 5242; www.willowtearooms. co.uk; Mon–Sat 9am–5pm, Sun 11am–5pm.
This is a faithful re-creation of the innovative design work Mackintosh carried out for well-known restaurateur Kate Cranston at the turn of the 20th century. The originals of the White Room and the Blue Room are in the care of Glasgow City Council. More Mackintosh interiors, afternoon tea and scones can be enjoyed at the other Willow Tea Rooms located at 217 Sauchiehall Street (tel: 0141-332 0521). ££

Tour 10

Excursion to Loch Lomond

An 80-mile (130km) foray into the Highlands, Loch Lomond and the Trossachs National Park, dipping into Britain's largest lake and visiting beguiling villages

You tak' the High Road,
and I'll tak' the Low Road,
and I'll be in Scotland afore ye.

The words of the Loch Lomond song distil the romance of the glens for Scots the world over, but for the most part, the reality of the High Road these days is a wide dual carriageway. Following signs for Crianlarich, the A82 continues westwards from Great Western Road in the centre of Glasgow along the north bank of the Clyde past Bowling, Dumbarton – the ancient capital of Strathclyde, with its castle on the rock – and Balloch.

This is a long excursion, but once at the loch, the roads mellow out and the countryside ranges from the lush and rolling to true Highland drama. The route includes points at which you

Highlights

- Balloch
- Drymen
- Balmaha
- Priory of Inchmahome
- Aberfoyle
- Loch Katrine

have to double back on yourself, but not for more than a few miles.

LUSS, ON THE BANKS OF LOCH LOMOND

The first is at Loch Lomond itself. Still following the Crianlarich signs, head first for the village of **Luss** ❶. Although surrounded on the outskirts by tourist services, the rose-clad cottages and the

Left: *peaceful Loch Lomond.*

old pier are attractive. On the other side of the main carriageway, a farm road signposted for Glen Luss runs up to some of the best hill-walking within easy reach of the city. A series of Corbetts (Scottish hills ranging between 2,500ft/762m and 3,000ft/914m) afford spectacular views to the Clyde estuary and the western islands. The weather in the mountains can change quickly, so always carry a map and dress warmly.

BALLOCH, DRYMEN AND BALMAHA

Returning south, turn left at the roundabout signed for **Balloch ❷** and left at the next roundabout. This leads into the heart of Loch Lomond's only town of any size. It hosts **Loch Lomond Shores** (tel: 01389-751 031; www. lochlomondshores.com; free), a visitor centre with shops, café and innovative aquarium (tel: 01389-721 500; charge) complete with sharks. Boats of all shapes and sizes crowd the banks and pontoons as the loch empties into the River Leven on its way to the Clyde.

The A811, signposted for Drymen, wanders through undulating farmland, passing only one village of note, **Gartocharn ❸**. The small hill at the back is called **Duncryne** and is worth the gentle climb for views of the water meadows of the southern loch, the wooded islands and the higher hills in the distance, including Ben Lomond.

At the junction with the A809, turn left to **Drymen ❹**, a delightful village 11 miles (18km) north of Glasgow. It retains a charming rural atmosphere. The cosy **Clachan Inn** (tel: 01360-660 824), established in 1734, is a good place to eat or enjoy a wee dram.

The B837 from the centre runs 5 miles (8km) to **Balmaha ❺**, a village lying on the Highland Boundary

ⓖ West Highland Way

The West Highland Way, a 95-mile (152km) walk from Milngavie, on the outskirts of Glasgow, to Fort William, starts at a granite obelisk in Douglas Street. The route follows ancient communication tracks as well as drove roads, military roads and disused railway tracks. The first 5-mile (8km) stage to Carbeth involves 500ft (148m) of ascent – a tame but enjoyable preamble to later challenges like climbing the Devil's Staircase below Glencoe's jagged Aonach Eagach ridge. See also www.west-highland-way.co.uk.

Above: the beautifully scenic terrain.

Above: Balmaha's boatyard is the place to pick up a loch cruiser.

Fault, separating the Highlands from the Lowlands. A scatter of white-washed houses surrounds the small inlet where **Balmaha's boatyard** (tel: 01360-870 214) caters for fishermen and loch cruisers, and offers places on the regular mailboat round the islands – an unusual day trip. The

Below: the historic Inchmahome priory, on the Lake of Menteith.

Oak Tree Inn (tel: 01360-870 357) is a good place to eat or stay. A path leads from the car park to Conic Hill; from the summit it is possible to see the 37 islands in the loch.

LAKE OF MENTEITH

Returning to Drymen, the A811 meanders north and east before joining the A81 north across the flatlands towards the hills of the Queen Elizabeth Forest. At the Rob Roy Motel, the route goes left to Aberfoyle, but turning right along the A81 for a short distance to the B8034 brings you to the island priory of **Inchmahome** ❻ (Apr–Sept daily 10am–4.30am, Oct daily 10am–3.30pm; charge includes ferry) on the Lake of Menteith, the only 'lake' in Scotland. These beautiful 12th-century Augustinian remains once sheltered Mary, Queen of Scots.

ABERFOYLE

Follow the A821 for the Trossachs. You'll next hit **Aberfoyle** ❼, a tourist honeypot. The road north negotiates a startling series of hairpins as it climbs past the **David Marshall Lodge** to Duke's Pass – watch for a kilted piper here in summer – then descends to Loch Achray. One of the small peaks on the far side of the loch is **Ben A'an** which affords a superb vista of Loch Katrine, Sir Walter Scott 's inspiration for *The Lady of the Lake* (1810).

Before Ben A'an, the main road branches off to **Loch Katrine 8**, where the steam yacht *Sir Walter Scott* sails on Glasgow's water supply (Apr–Oct; call to check times; tel: 01877-332 000/376 316). Bikes are available

Above: the banks of Loch Katrine are ideal for a peaceful bicycle ride.

to hire for a ride along the loch road. For the quickest way back to Glasgow, travel 10 miles (16km) to Callander, then on to Stirling to join the M9.

ⓔ Eating Out

Balloch
Balloch House Vintage Inn
Balloch Road; tel: 01389-752 579; daily lunch and dinner.
Serves hearty fish and chips alongside more adventurous dishes. £

Near Balloch
Cameron House Hotel
A82; tel: 01389-755 565; www.devere hotels.co.uk; Cameron Grill: daily breakfast and dinner; Martin Wishart's: Wed–Fri dinner, Sat–Sun lunch/dinner.

This luxurious lochside former stately home offers several dining options including Martin Wishart's Michelin-starred eatery, which serves delicious dishes such as turbot with sweet garlic cannelloni. £–£££
Duck Bay Marina
tel: 01389-751 234; www.duckbay. co.uk; daily lunch and dinner.
This modern hotel has large picture windows with glorious loch views. Expect classics like cullen skink, plus pasta dishes and crêpes. ££

Loch Lomond

Everyone has heard of it, but the loch bit of Loch Lomond is just one of the shimmering jewels in what is Scotland's most famous and diversified national park

OUTDOOR TREATS

Loch Lomond and the Trossachs National Park stretches a little west of the loch, north to Tyndrum, east to Callander and south to Balloch. Straddling the West Highland fault line, the heather-clad hills abound with 'darksome glens and gleaming lochs', as wrote legendary Scottish author Sir Walter Scott.

This area has a magnetism for walkers, cyclists and those who love water sports. Loch Lomond and the Trossachs National Park Gateway Centre in Balloch (www.loch lomond-trossachs.org) has every kind of information about the park, including geological history, walking routes, cycle paths and details about all the guides and companies who provide tours, mountain-bike excursions, horse riding, fishing and boat trips on the lochs (notably the *Sir Walter Scott* steamer on Loch Katrine; see p.103).

WALKING COUNTRY

There are a multitude of easy and short walks, such as the **Creag an Tuirc** walk, which begins at Balquidder (2.5 miles/4km, about 2 hours), and the hillier **Cruach Tairbeirt** walk (4.7 miles/7.5km, about 3 hours),

Flora and Fauna

As you travel away from the sparkling shores of the loch, you're greeted by spectacular hills, glens with densely wooded forests and a real sense that you're surrounded by the wild. The national park boasts 200 species of birds, including buzzards, ospreys, golden eagles, peregrine falcons, pied flycatchers, and capercaillies – although you're more likely to hear the cricking noise of these than see them among the heathery thickets. The park is home to 25 percent of Britain's wild plant species: there are 500 flowering species and ferns, with rarities such as wood anemone, wood sorrel and, magnificent in May, thick blankets of bluebells. As for fauna, take your time and keep quiet and you have some chance of being in the presence of – if not seeing – red deer, polecats, pine martens and wildcats. Meanwhile, Loch Lomond is the largest freshwater loch in the UK; within it swim salmon, pike and powan, a whitefish only found in one other place.

taking you up to 1,485ft (450m). In exchange for your efforts you receive glorious views of Loch Lomond – weather permitting.

If you must climb a hill, try **Ben Ledi**, classified as a Corbett, a smaller set of Scottish hills (5 miles/8km, about 4 hours). It might be wee but on a clear day you can see the Firth of Forth from the summit at 2,508ft (760m). For those craving to bag a Munro, Scotland's highest peaks, 3,465ft (1,050m) -high **Ben Lui** (13 miles/21km, about 7 hours) is a must-climb. For much of the year its Coire Gaothaich (Windy Corrie) is filled with snow, lending it an alpine character. Ben Lui is reached from Tyndrum.

For those with time, the inclination and broken-in boots, the famous **West Highland Way** (92½ miles/148km, up to 2,650ft/800m) from Milngavie to Fort William is one of the most trampled and loved walks in Scotland. It takes between 7 and 10 days.

Whatever walk you choose to do, be prepared for a dramatic change in the weather, even in the warmest months, and have proper footwear, a map and compass (the ability to use these properly is a must too!) as well as waterproof clothing. Also, leave word of your plans with your accommodation.

Above: the Loch Lomond park is perfect walking country. **Top Left**: a Loch Lomond walkway. **Centre Left**: a local pine marten. **Bottom Left**: the rare, vocally impressive capercaillie, a woodland grouse.

Excursion to Clyde Valley

Two country parks, riverside walks, the David Livingstone Centre, Craignethan Castle and fascinating New Lanark make this a stimulating jaunt

Highlights

- Strathclyde Country Park
- Duke of Hamilton's Mausoleum
- David Livingstone Centre
- Chatelherault Country Park
- Craignethan Castle
- Lanark
- New Lanark

The River Clyde, the wonderful Clyde, The name of it thrills me and fills me with pride.

When Glaswegians sing praise of the river that gave their city meaning, they think of the clatter of shipyards and the sway of giant cranes. But further down the valley is an altogether different river, wandering through gentle hills and watering fertile orchards and fruit farms. This 45-mile (70km) tour requires a car, or a bike for the very fit, taking in country parks, lots of intriguing history and a Unesco World Heritage Site at New Lanark.

STRATHCLYDE COUNTRY PARK

The M8 snakes through the centre of Glasgow, and it is possible to join it at many points. Once on the eastbound carriageway, follow signs for Carlisle and Edinburgh through the industrial eastern suburbs until you reach junction 8 with the M73, then follow signs for Carlisle.

Off the A723 between a cluster of Glasgow's satellite towns – including **Hamilton** and **Motherwell** – is

Left: the picturesque Falls of Clyde.
Above: there are thrills of all sorts at Strathclyde Country Park.

Strathclyde Country Park ❶. It's accessible via junction 5 of the M74. This huge recreation area includes a man-made loch that offers sailing, windsurfing and water-skiing, along with an amusement park, **M&D's** (tel: 01698-333 777; www.scotlands themepark.com) featuring some of the biggest rides in Scotland.

The **Low Parks Museum** (tel: 01698-328 232; Mon–Sat 10am–5pm, Sun noon–5pm; free), built on the site of the Hamilton Palace, complete with a mezzanine café, is located on Muir Street. It tells the turbulent history of the town, its regiment – the Cameronians – and the Hamilton family, whose spectacular **Mausoleum ❷**, built by the 10th Duke in the 1840s, has impassive stone lions guarding the enormous bronze doors and beautiful marblework within.

DAVID LIVINGSTONE CENTRE

A few miles up the A724 at Blantyre is the **David Livingstone Centre ❸**

(tel: 0844-493 2207; www.nts.org.uk; Apr–Dec Mon–Sat 10am–5pm, Sun 12.30pm–5pm; charge), a memorial to Scotland's greatest missionary explorer, who was born here in 1813. Brought up as a poor factory boy, he led an eventful life which included the discovery of the Victoria Falls on the border between Zambia and Zimbabwe while on a journey across the African continent in 1855. He died of dysentery in 1873 while searching for the then unknown source of the River Nile.

CHATELHERAULT COUNTRY PARK

Returning through Hamilton, join the A72 for Lanark and, as the suburbs give way to countryside, the gates of **Chatelherault Country Park ❹** (tel: 01698-426 213; Mon–Sat 10am–5pm, Sun noon–5.30pm) open up on the right. A visitor centre, once the kennels for the hunting dogs of the Duke of Hamilton, butts onto the main building, designed by William Adam for the Fifth Duke and completed in 1744. The building fell into dereliction – mining subsidence has added a jaunty slope to some floors – but a masterful restoration was completed in 1987 allowing visitors to fullly appreciate the superb plasterwork with its ornate figures from classical mythology.

Above: the fascinating New Lanark is a Unesco World Heritage Site.

ⓖ Riverside Walks

Chatelherault Country Park consists of nearly 500 acres (200 hectares) of the Avon Gorge, one of the least polluted of the Clyde's tributaries. There are miles of riverside walks and picturesque sights here including the dramatic Duke's Bridge, the medieval mystery of Cadzow Castle and rolling parkland featuring cattle whose lineage dates back to Roman times.

Above: the Chatelherault Country Park is packed with bucolic charm.

CRAIGNETHAN CASTLE

The A72 now follows the twists and turns of the Clyde as it runs through a valley of soft-fruit, tomato and vegetable growers, past Dalserf's 1655 church and the pretty half-timbered village of Rosebank with its three-star Popinjay Hotel (tel: 01555-860 441). Slightly further on, a sign points right to **Craignethan Castle** ⓣ (Apr–Sept Mon–Sun 9.30am–6.30pm, 1 Nov–31 Mar Sat–Sun 9.30am–4.30pm; charge), a sombre keep situated 2 miles (3km) up a narrow and twisting road. Dating back to around 1530, this rambling ruin was one of the last great family tower fortresses, and from it the Hamilton family played a pivotal role in Scottish politics, including supporting Mary, Queen of Scots, whom they sheltered here after her abdication in 1567.

Although Sir Walter Scott denied that its ivy-clad ruins were the inspiration for Tillietudlem Castle in the Waverley novel *Old Mortality* – and indeed he is said to have considered settling here instead of Abbotsford – its remote location and air of mystery are resonant for many of Claverhouse and the Covenanting bands.

LANARK AND NEW LANARK

Back on the A72, the road continues through Kirkfieldbank to the historic town of **Lanark**, a slope trodden during the Wars of Independence (1286–1328) by the raggle-taggle hordes of William Wallace, whose statue looks down from an 18th-century church along a bustling main street divided by pretty floral displays. This busy market town was founded in 1140 by King David. He established a castle here, long since disappeared.

Following the signs at the top of the street for New Lanark, the road twists down again to the Clyde and one of the most remarkable episodes in Scotland's industrial history, as well as one of its most adventurous heritage restoration projects. At first sight, **New Lanark ❻** (tel: 01555-661 345; www. newlanark.org; Apr–Oct 10am–5pm, Nov–Mar 10am–4pm; charge) seems little more than a group of stone-built warehouses, but it was here that David Dale and his son-in-law Robert Owen conducted a social experiment that was to have lasting repercussions for the bitterly oppressed working classes.

Dale, from Stewarton, made his fortune in weaving and French yarns. In 1785, using the abundant water power of the Clyde, he set up the New Lanark Mills which, at their height, employed over 2,000 workers, many of them children. Along with Owen,

who assumed management in 1799, he introduced a regime of decent housing, reasonable wages, education and healthcare, to prove his theory that contented workers were productive workers. His message did as much to create a social revolution as the mills had done for industry, and as a result workers' rights began to be considered seriously elsewhere.

The village, now a Unesco World Heritage Site, has been restored as a living community complete with hotel and shops, and the millworkers' tenement rows are desirable properties. There is also a youth hostel here (tel: 01555-666 710). In the Visitor Centre, various audiovisual rides show life in the mill past, present and future.

Along the river, a sylvan walk leads to the **Falls of Clyde**, where the Scottish Wildlife Trust organises badger watches and the keen-eyed may spot kingfishers, owls and pipistrelle bats as night descends.

Below: the handsome hunting lodge at Chatelherault Country Park has been sensitively restored.

Tour 12

Excursion to Burns Country

On the trail of poet Robert Burns, visiting auld hair and Rabbie-raising haunts – including the Bachelors' Club and Burns Cottage, his birthplace

For a' that, an' a' that,
It's coming yet for a' that,
That Man to Man, the world o'er,
Shall brothers be for a' that

Scots, with their tradition of struggle for social justice, embrace the egalitarian theme that runs through the works of their National Bard, Robert 'Rabbie' Burns (1759–96). The memory of his turbulent life is kept alive at Burns Suppers across the world at the end of January. Burns's associations with Glasgow were tenuous – minor dealings with publishers – but the literary legacy he left and the memorials to his origins in Burns Country are easily accessible from the city. A car is required for this excursion to the southwest coast taking in the various Burns-related monuments and sights.

Highlights

- Burns House, Mauchline
- Highland Mary Monument
- Bachelors' Club
- Ayr
- Burns National Heritage Park
- Burns Cottage
- Auld Alloway Kirk
- Brig O'Doon
- Souter Johnnie's Cottage

MAUCHLINE AND FAILFORD

Leave the city on the M8 westbound and join the M77, then the A77 towards Ayr. Turn off just after Kilmarnock on to the A76 (signposted

Left: Crossraguel Abbey, dusted with snow. **Above**: Burns' old hangout, the Bachelors' Club.

BACHELORS' CLUB

Past Failford, a brief diversion on the right leads to Tarbolton, where the National Trust for Scotland is the custodian of the **Bachelors' Club ❸** (tel: 0844-493 2146; 1 Apr–30 Sept Fri–Tue 1–5pm, last admission 4.30pm; morning visits available for pre-booked groups; charge). The 17th-century thatched house just off the main road is where the poet and his cronies formed a debating club with, it has to be said, easy access to the inn next door. It was here that Burns was introduced to the Freemasonry that shaped his philosophy of the brotherhood of Man.

Returning to the B743, it is 6 miles (10km) to **Ayr ❹**, a resort town with sandy beaches and a statue of Burns in the main square. Crossing the main road over the River Ayr, the 15th-century pedestrian bridge on the left is

Dumfries). This road leads through typical Ayrshire countryside to the village of Mauchline, on the outskirts of which stands the Scots baronial folly of the **National Burns Memorial Tower**, established in 1896. The **Burns House ❶** (tel: 01387-255 297; Apr–Sept Mon–Sat 10am–5pm, Sun 2–5pm, Oct–Mar Tue–Sat 10am–1pm, 2–5pm; free) in which the poet lived is in the village centre, as is **Poosie Nansie's Tavern**, said to have inspired part of *The Jolly Beggars*.

Leaving the village on the B743, the road winds towards **Failford ❷**, a scatter of houses in a small dip. A path behind a sign to Failford Gorge – easy to miss – leads to a monument to **Highland Mary**, the mysterious but beautiful woman for whom Burns wrote *My Highland Lassie O*. This is one of the lesser Burns monuments, but the inscription on the pillar is touching:

> *That sacred hour can I forget,*
> *Can I forget the hallowed grove,*
> *Where by the winding Ayr we met,*
> *To live one day of parting love.*

Above: the spooky graveyard at Auld Alloway Kirk.

the **Auld Brig** and the pillared steeple straight ahead is Ayr Town Hall. Burns was baptised in the Auld Kirk.

ROBERT BURNS BIRTHPLACE MUSEUM

Heading out of town on the A719 (signposted for Maidens), look for a sign for the Heads of Ayr then turn left at the first sign for **Alloway**, a pretty village of rose-entwined cottages that

ⓖ Burns by Bike

During the summer months Cycle Ayrshire (tel: 01290-550 276; www. cycleayrshire.co.uk) organises Burns by Bike outings led by expert riders over mainly minor roads. Various excursions cater for all abilities, including beginners and families. The more taxing 38-mile (60km) ride starts at Rozelle Park in Ayr, then takes in Tarbolton Mauchline, Coylton and Dalrymple before returning to Ayr. A decent level of fitness is suggested for this ride.

is at the heart of Burns Country. A car park on the left at the junction with the B7024 to Maybole serves the **Burns National Heritage Park**, which includes **Burns Cottage**, the poet's birthplace, and the new **Robert Burns Birthplace Museum** ⑤ (tel: 0844-493 2601; www.burnsmuseum. org.uk; Apr–Sept daily 10am–5.30pm, Oct–Mar daily 10am–5pm; charge), which opened in 2011. His birthplace is a clay wall-and-thatch house, which the poet's father William built and where he instilled young Robert's love of language and learning. The new museum contains the most important collection of Burns's work, including the original copy of the *Kilmarnock Edition*, the first collection of poems he published to raise cash in order to emigrate to Jamaica. The state-of-the-art technology aims to bring the life, loves and demons of the poet to life. As well as these permanent collections there are a variety of temporary exhibitions of Burns-related art, and poetry readings and musical events. There are also tours of the site with expert guides to tell the history of Burns and the area.

Auld Alloway Kirk, also in the complex but just a little further on, is a 16th-century refuge that was a ruin even in Burns's day and was last used in 1756. Its gloomy graveyard holds the remains of Burns's father, and the mossy crypts and worn stones with their goblin carvings are a suitably chilling setting for the dance of the witches as the Devil – '*a tousie tyke, black, grim and large*' – played the pipes and '*gart them skirl*'.

When Tam, inspired by John Barleycorn, interrupted their dance with the shout: '*Weel done, Cutty Sark*', his mare Meg fled to **Brig O'Doon** nearby to escape minus '*her ain grey tail*'. This 13th-century cobbled bridge with its ancient arch now stands below the **Burns Monument**, a Grecian tower designed by Thomas Hamilton and opened in 1823.

TOWARDS SOUTH AYRSHIRE

The B7024 carries on to **Maybole**, where Burns's father and mother met in 1756. Joining the A77, signposted for Stranraer, the road leads past the 13th-century ruins of **Crossraguel Abbey** ❻ with its abbot's tower and dovecote, to the village of Kirkoswald. Here the National Trust for Scotland maintains the thatched **Souter Johnnie's Cottage** ❼ (tel: 0844-493 2147; Apr–Sept Fri–Tue 11.30am–5pm; charge), a representation of the daily life of the cobbler who was the inspiration behind Tam O'Shanter's '*ancient, trusty, drouthy crony*'.

This is a long but fascinating run. Finish with drinks at the **Westin Turnberry Resort Hotel** (tel: 01655-331 000), scene of so many memorable moments in Open golf history.

Eating Out

Ayr
Fouters Bistro
2a Academy Street; tel: 01292-261 391; Tue–Sat lunch and dinner.
In the vaults of an old bank, this renowned place serves excellent dishes using quality ingredients such as Gressingham duck, Ayrshire lamb and John Dory. ££

Below: Burns Cottage, the birthplace of the beloved Scottish bard.

Active Pursuits

For all its municipal grandeur and urban chic, this 'dear green place' is surrounded by hills and water and full of things to do.

Walkers are less than an hour away from the splendours of Loch Lomond and the Trossachs National Park *(see feature p.104)*, which has Munros, Corbetts, heather hill rambles, forest walks and nature trails that will allow you to glimpse some of the 500 species of flowering plant and 250 species of bird that reside here. For the really serious outdoors enthusiast, there's the West Highland Way to explore, which takes about five to seven days to walk. It takes you from Milngavie, just north of Glasgow, to Fort William, a distance of 92 miles (148km), passing through some of Scotland's most stunning scenery. For information on all the walks that can be done in this area, visit www. lochlomond-trossachs.org.

BOATING

Glasgow is a city built on its maritime might, but it's only in recent years that marinas and boat clubs have really started to pop up. Sail out of the Firth of Clyde and head north along the shores and you will

Above: cycling along a canal towpath.

be gobsmacked by the beauty of the sea lochs, rocky outcrops and inlets, not to mention the isles of Islay and Mull. Experienced sailors should visit www.westcoastboating.org for information on all the routes, charts, sites, nature and companies that offer boats for hire. For those who can't sail but want to go out on the open waves, the *Waverley* (www.waverley excursions.co.uk) is the last remaining seagoing paddle steamer in the world and does summer sails along the Clyde, as well as to the northern lochs and nearby islands of Arran, Bute and Mull.

Previous Pages: natural splendours await for those keen to get active.
Left: the PS *Waverley* paddle steamer.
Above: boating is popular.

CYCLING

There are lots of cycle paths around Glasgow and along the Clyde. Within the city, the Glasgow Mountain Bike Circuit in Pollok Park has a green circuit for those wanting a gentle ride through the woods, a blue circuit for a bit of bounce and climb, and a red circuit for those who want really rugged terrain. You can rent a bike from www.cosybike.co.uk.

FISHING

One benefit of the demise of heavy industry is that the Clyde is less polluted now, and trout and salmon have returned. Angling is becoming increasingly popular on the banks of the rivers of Glasgow. The United Clyde Angling Protective Association Ltd looks after the Clyde and its tributaries, and you can buy a permit from local tackle shops to fish on a particular stretch.

Ⓕ Football's Old Firm

Football fans will associate Glasgow with its two big teams, Celtic and Rangers. The rivalry between the Old Firm (as they are collectively known) is embedded in the history of the city and passions are as fiery as ever – joint initiatives to confront its nastier side continue. Celtic Park, otherwise known as Parkhead (or Paradise), is in the East End (www.celticfc.co.uk), while Rangers, who were forced to begin their 2012 season in the lowly ranks of the Scottish third division after going into administration, make their home at Ibrox in the Southside (www.rangers.co.uk). Both clubs offer stadium tours.

Above: Old Firm clashes are notorious for their intensity.

Above: playing a few holes at the Pollok Golf Club, with the impressive Pollok House in the background.

GOLF

There are dozens of golf courses in and around Glasgow. Douglas Park (tel: 0141-942 0985; www.douglas parkgolfclub.co.uk) is an attractive 18-hole course north of the city near Milngavie. Lethamhill (tel: 0141-276 0810; junction 8 off the M8) is a municipal 18-hole course overlooking Hogganfield Loch.

HORSE RIDING

There are a few horse-riding centres around the outskirts of Glasgow. Easterton Stables in Milngavie (www. eastertonstables.co.uk) offers lessons, or, if you can already handle a horse, you can hack along the dips and dells of Mugdock Country Park in the Campsie Fells, surely one of the most delightful ways to see the scenery.

Ⓚ Children's Activities

Glasgow is a city with activities for all ages. At **Hampden Park** (tel: 0141-616 6139; www.scottishfoot-ballmuseum.org.uk; Mon–Sat 10am–5pm, Sun 11am–5pm), Scotland's national football stadium, kids and adults alike will enjoy the Scottish Football Hall of Fame, and have an opportunity to tour the stadium.

Kelburne Country Park, which is located near Largs (tel: 01475-568 685), boasts waterfalls, falconry displays, an assault course and 'The Secret Forest'. The refurbished **Summerlee Heritage Trust** at Coatbridge (tel: 01236-638 460) offers kids the chance to ride on an old tram as part of Scotland's only

electric-driven tramway. Also out this way, the **Time Capsule** (tel: 01236-449 572; www.thetime-capsule.info), with swimming and ice-skating among volcanoes and cavemen, is worth a visit.

Above: a falconry demonstration at Kelburne Country Park.

Themed Holidays

Whether you have a day, a weekend or a week, Glasgow is full of opportunities to learn a new skill or to do something useful.

Artistic breaks

Glasgow School of Art (tel: 0141-353 4500; www.gsa.ac.uk) is the alma mater of many of Britain's edgiest artists, such as Roddy Buchanan, Nathan Coley and Christine Borland. During July, the school runs a summer course allowing you to learn and work alongside resident lecturers and guest artists located in a number of the studios across the campus, including the famous painting studios in the Charles Rennie Mackintosh Building. You can also book cheap accommodation within the student halls of residence (en-suite accommodation at Margaret Macdonald House).

Bagpiping

If you've ever dreamed of mastering the bagpipes, you can learn to pipe at the **College of Piping** (tel: 0141-334-3587; www.college-of-piping.co.uk). There are day and week-long courses at hugely attractive prices at the centrally located school.

Buddhist retreats

If you feel the need for inner peace, you have a good chance of finding it at **Kagyu Samye Ling** (tel: 01387-373 232; www.samyeling.org), Europe's oldest Tibetan Buddhist monastery. A range of retreats and courses cover all aspects of the practice. The monastery is a two-hour drive from Glasgow or 90 minutes by train.

Cooking classes

The **Cookery School** (tel: 0141-552 5239; www.thecookeryschool. org) at Peckham's in Glassford Street offers even the most hopeless cooks a chance to learn how to bring food together in a tasty and attractive way. Choose from a one-day course in Italian cookery (making minestrone and pesto among other dishes), up to a full five-day course of cooking, eating and drinking.

Nature

The National Trust for Scotland's **Thistle Camps** (www.nts.org.uk/ThistleCamps) recruit volunteers to repair upland and lowland footpaths, control rhododendron growth and erect fencing. You can even learn how to restore bogs in the estates and properties of the NTS, which include the likes of Ben Lawers, Ben Lomond and Brodick Castle in Arran. A week's volunteering includes basic accommodation and food.

Above: learn to play the most Scottish instrument of all at the College of Piping.

Practical Information

GETTING THERE

By air

Glasgow has an excellent international airport to the west at Abbotsinch (tel: 0844-481 5555), which is served by flights from all main UK airports and has connections to Europe and North America. It has direct motorway links to the city centre, a journey of about 15 minutes. A taxi to the city centre costs around £20 from a rank outside the terminal building. Frequent Service 500 buses (Glasgow Flyer Airport Express), which cost £5 one way and £7 return, connect with Glasgow Central (15 mins) and Buchanan Bus Station (25 mins). The Paisley Gilmour Street Railway Station is closest to the airport; around eight trains an hour depart for the city centre.

British Airways and British Midland operate shuttle flights from London. British Airways (tel: 0870-850 9850; www.britishairways.com) operates flights from Heathrow and Gatwick. Flybe (tel: 0871-700 2000; www.flybe.com) has flights from Belfast and Manchester. Easyjet (tel: 0870-600 0000; www.easyjet.com) connects Glasgow with Stansted, Luton and Gatwick, as well as Bristol, Belfast and the European hub of Paris Charles de Gaulle. Ryanair (tel: 0870-728 0280; www.ryanair.com) operates from Stansted to Prestwick, which is about 40 minutes south of Glasgow near Ayr but has efficient road and rail links. There are also direct flights available to various other UK, European and North American destinations. For details of flights, and to book tickets online, visit www.glasgowairport.com and www.glasgowprestwick.com.

By car

From the south, the west-coast route follows the M1 to Birmingham, then the M6 to the Scottish border, then the A74 and M74, which joins the M8 into the city. The slower east-coast route follows the M1 and A1 into Edinburgh, then the cross-country M8 to Glasgow. From the north, the A9 joins the M9 near Stirling and then the M80, A80 and M8 into Glasgow.

By coach

National Express (tel: 08717-818 178; www.nationalexpress.com) runs a regular coach service from all points in England and Wales into Buchanan Bus Station.

By rail

Virgin Trains (tel: 08719-774222; www.virgintrains.co.uk) currently operates the main west-coast route from London, Birmingham and Manchester, but the running of the franchise will

Below: the Clyde Arc, also known as 'Squinty Bridge', was opened to vehicle traffic in 2007.

Above: pedestrian walkways make it straightforward to get around on foot.

be up for negotiation again in 2013. Queen Street Station has a shuttle to Edinburgh and serves the north. For general rail enquiries in Glasgow and Scotland: tel: 0845-484 950; www. firstgroup.com/scotrail. Buy tickets online at www.thetrainline.com.

GETTING AROUND
On foot
A colour-coded sign system facilitates navigation of the city centre and main visitor areas. Distinctive blue panels provide directions and information about sights, maps and pedestrian routes. The Glasgow Tourist Informa-tion Centre on George Square *(see p.123)* has decent free maps and some more detailed ones for a few pounds.

By public transport
Glasgow's subway network is one of the oldest in the world, but 15 stations on a 24-minute circular track mean that no journey will take longer than 12 minutes. Packages are available, such as the Family Day Tripper Tickets (unlimited travel on First Scotrail serv-ices, subway, some ferries and many bus operators). A single ticket costs £1.20. The subway's 'Discovery' ticket is good value: for £3.50 you can enjoy one day's unlimited travel after 9.30am Monday to Saturday and all day Sunday.

Above ground, First Scotrail (www. firstgroup.com/scotrail) runs the ex-tensive rail network. Glasgow Central Station serves the South and England while Queen Street Station handles trains to and from Edinburgh and the north. City Sightseeing Glasgow runs open-air bus tours from George Square. National Express, Citylink and Megabus coach companies operate out of Buchanan Street Bus Station.

Car hire and parking
Glasgow city-centre traffic is heavy, but a car is useful for excursions to out-lying areas. Car-hire firms in Glasgow include: **Arnold Clark** (tel: 0141-954 1963), **Avis** (tel: 0844-581 0147) and **Europcar** (tel: 0141-249 4106).

ⓖ Cycling
There are great cycle paths, includ-ing the 21-mile (34km) Glasgow to Loch Lomond Cycleway, from Bell's Bridge, beside the Clyde Audito-rium on the Clyde, to Balloch. Bikes are carried free on all Strathclyde Passenger Transport-supported rail services. For information on cycle routes, visit www.sustrans.org.uk, tel: 0845-113 0065, or ask for the *Clyde and Loch Lomond Cycleway* leaflet at the tourist office.

Above: Glasgow and its surrounding area has many clear cycle paths.

Car parks are plentiful but busy, with spaces around St Enoch Square filled by mid-morning. Multistorey car parks are at Mitchell Street, Cambridge Street, Montrose Street, Waterloo Street, Oswald Street and Buchanan Galleries. Unauthorised parking is not advisable, as tow-away trucks and clamping units abound. If your accommodation is in the West End, take the subway into the city centre.

Steamer and seaplane

The world's last surviving paddle steamer, the PS *Waverley* (tel: 0845-130 4647), makes its home berth at Pacific Quay by Glasgow Science Centre. A relic of the great days of steam, its massive engines are still open for inspection on summer cruises down the Firth of Clyde to Rothesay, Arran and the Kyles of Bute (www.waverley excursions.co.uk).

For a breathtaking flight over Loch Lomond, Tobermory, Oban and the west coast, charter a Loch Lomond Seaplane (tel: 01436-675 030; www. lochlomondseaplanes.com). Planes take off from a purpose-built dock by the Glasgow Science Centre.

Above: a vintage transport sign.

Taxis

Black taxis are licensed by Glasgow City Council and can be flagged down in the street, but there are also many private taxi firms which are slightly cheaper.

FACTS FOR THE VISITOR

Disabled travellers

The Glasgow Tourist Information Centre dispenses advice and leaflets for disabled travellers. The city's main sights have improved provision and access in recent years. For information on disabled access regarding hotels and other businesses, consult www.disabledgo.com.

Emergencies

Fire, Police, Ambulance: tel: 999
Fire HQ: (north of the river) Port Dundas Road, tel: 0141-302 3222; (south of the river) McFarlane Street, tel: 0141-445 2223
Strathclyde Police HQ: 173 Pitt Street, tel: 0141-532 2000
Royal Infirmary: Castle Street, tel: 0141-211 4000
Western Infirmary: Dumbarton Road, tel: 0141-211 2000

Opening hours

City centre shops are generally open 9am–5.30pm (Mon–Sat). Many stores

Left: a Loch Lomond seaplane returns to land at its floating dock in Glasgow.

stay open later – some until 8pm – on a Thursday. Sunday opening is now common in the city centre: noon–5pm is the norm.

Most major banks open 9.30am–4.30pm weekdays; some open Saturday mornings until 12.30pm.

Postal services

Most post offices are open Monday to Friday 9am to 5.30pm, and Saturday 9am to 12.30–1pm. For help and advice on all post office counter services, tel: 08457-223 344; www.postoffice.co.uk.

Tourist information

The **Glasgow Tourist Information Centre**, 11 George Square (tel: 0141-204 4400; www.seeglasgow.com; May, June and Sept Mon–Sat 9am–7pm, July–Aug 9am–8pm, Oct–Apr 9am–6pm, all year Sun 10am–6pm), provides practical guidance on getting around the city and the surrounding areas. Staff are on hand to help with information on the vast range of tours available, the city's historical and cultural attractions, as well as providing an accommodation

Above: crowds at the busy Queen Street train station.

booking service. There's also a small shop on site.

Bureaux de change can be found at **American Express** (66 Gordon Street, tel: 0141-225 2905) and **Thomas Cook** (15–17 Gordon Street, tel: 0844-335 7296).

🌈 Gay and Lesbian Scene

Glasgow has a thriving gay scene and is home to Scotland's biggest gay festival, Glasgay! (Sept–Nov), which encompasses everything from film to club nights. Glasgay's **Q! Gallery** (27–9 Trongate; tel: 0141-552 7575; www.qgallery.org; Mon–Fri 11am–5pm) showcases art and has a bookstore. Popular gay-lesbian hangouts are centred on the Merchant City and include **Delmonica's** (68 Virginia Street; tel: 0141-552 4803) for food, cabaret and club nights; and **Underground Bar** (6a John Street; tel: 0141-553 2456), a stylish place big

on home-cooked food and friendliness. For more information and latest listings check out www.glasgay.co.uk and www.thescottishgayscene.co.uk.

Above: girls' night out.

Accommodation

Glasgow's hotels range from the swanky and expensive to cosy B&Bs housed in handsome Victorian houses. New boutique hotels – some contemporary-style new-builds and others imaginative conversions of historic buildings – have been added in recent years, which have upped the standards generally. Look out for the new luxury hotel and spa, The Hamilton, currently being incorporated into the old BBC building and due to open in 2013. The Glasgow Tourist Information Centre *(see p.123)* provides an accommodation booking service.

Prices of hotels listed here vary seasonally; the ranges below (quoted as a guide only) suggest prices for one night in a double room on a bed-and-breakfast basis in peak season:

££££	over £150
£££	£100–150
££	£60–100
£	under £60

CENTRAL GLASGOW AND MERCHANT CITY

ABode Glasgow
129 Bath Street; tel: 0141-221 6789; www.abodehotels.co.uk.
Located in an elegant Edwardian Bath Street building which once housed the atmospheric Arthouse Hotel. New landlords ABode have added mainstream design touches and modern comforts. ££

Brunswick Hotel
106–8 Brunswick Street; tel: 0141-552 0001; www.brunswickhotel.co.uk.
In the heart of the Merchant City quarter, this stylish hotel is extremely good value in terms of both location and elegance. There's also an on-site Italian café-cum-restaurant. ££

Hotel du Vin at One Devonshire Gardens
1 Devonshire Gardens, Great Western Road; tel: 0141-339 2001; www.hotelduvin.com.
Luxury accommodation in an elegant tree-lined terrace comprising five sandstone houses. Quality and comfort abound, from the Egyptian cotton bedding to the Whisky Snug and its 'Glasgow Restaurant of the Year'-winning eatery. ££££

Radisson SAS Hotel
301 Argyle Street; tel: 0141-204 3333; www.radissonsas.com.
Around the corner from Glasgow Central Station, the jaw-dropping glass-fronted lobby area impresses anyone interested in contemporary design. The cavernous art-filled atrium bar is a social hub, while the Collage bar and restaurant has picked up awards. Standard modern rooms can seem a tad dull but the corner suites are gorgeous. ££

Above: a truly luxurious bathing experience at the Hotel du Vin at One Devonshire Gardens.

Above: the stylish bar at ABode Glasgow.

WEST END AND BY THE CLYDE

Alamo Guest House
46 Gray Street, Kelvingrove; tel: 0141-339 2395; www.alamoguesthouse.com.
A popular family-run hotel opposite Kelvingrove Park set in a grand terraced house. The cosy rooms are simply furnished, well maintained and offer great value. £

Crowne Plaza Glasgow
Congress Road; tel: 0871-423 4896; www.ichotelsgroup.com.
Modern high-rise by the Clyde, situated beside the SECC, offering a range of functional rooms and suites, a grand reception with bar-restaurant and shop, and a pool. £££

Hilton Garden Inn
Finnieston Quay; tel: 0141-240 1002; www.hiltongardeninn.hilton.com.
A stylish yet comfortable place to stay next to the Clyde, with a fresh contemporary design and beguiling café-bar with views of the river from the terrace. Free Wi-fi in every room. ££

Kelvin Hotel
15 Buckingham Terrace; tel: 0141-339 7143; www.kelvinhotel.com.
Family-owned hotel in the West End within an impressive Victorian building. Guest rooms have high ceilings and free Wi-fi. The Kelvin apartment sleeps up to four and is ideal for families. £

SOUTHSIDE

Glasgow Guest House
56 Dumbrek Road, near Pollok Park; tel: 0141-427 0129; www.glasgow-guest-house.co.uk.
This bed and breakfast offers homely accommodation and is handy for the parks detailed in Tour 8 *(p.86)* and the airport. £

Mar Hall
Earl of Mar Estate, Renfrew; tel: 0141-812 9999; www.marhall.com.
Stunning Gothic mansion located 10 minutes west of Glasgow airport in Renfrewshire. Comfy rooms and suites come in calming hues. The Aveda Spa offers treatments and gym facilities. ££££

Number 10
10–12 Queen's Drive; tel: 0141-424 0160; www.10hotel.co.uk.
The long-established Dunkeld Hotel has been spruced up, rejigging the layout to make many rooms more spacious. Expect warm hospitality and professional service. ££

Sherbrooke Castle Hotel

11 Sherbrooke Avenue, Pollokshields; tel: 0141-427 4227; www.sherbrooke. co.uk.

A Victorian mock-Gothic pile complete with baronial turrets near Pollok Park. Tartan carpets, period furnishings and antiques give the public areas a cosy atmospheric feel, while guest rooms have modern bathrooms, warmth and free Wi-fi. ££

NORTH OF THE CITY

Cameron House Hotel

Loch Lomond; tel: 01389-755 565; www.deverehotels.co.uk.

This five-star hotel is housed in a luxurious baronial-style mansion in a stunning Loch Lomond waterside setting. There are first-class spa and golf facilities, and you can even arrive by seaplane. ££££

Dakota Eurocentral

Eurocentral Junction of the A8/M8; tel: 01698-835 444; www.dakota hotels.co.uk

A stylish yet cosy hotel with lots of contemporary design touches and useful high-tech facilities, including free Wi-fi. The award-winning bar and grill serves Scottish fish dishes and the sweetest oysters from Borough Market in London. ££

Red Deer Vintage Inn

1 Auchenkilns Park, Cumbernauld; tel: 01236-795 861; www.vintageinn. co.uk/thereddeercumbernauld.

Great-value accommodation with functional, clean rooms and a pub-style restaurant. Popular with anglers who cast off at nearby Broadward Loch. The Vintage Inns chain also has a hotel at Balloch near Loch Lomond. ££

WEBSITES

For a comprehensive list of hotels in the city, see www.glasgowguide.co.uk/hotels.html.

Guesthouses/Bed & Breakfasts: www.information-britain.co.uk; www.scottishaccommodationindex. com; www.laterooms.com

Green: www.organicholidays.co.uk; www.ecofriendlytourist.com

Self-catering: For those staying for more than a few days, an apartment is a sensible option:
www.citybaseapartments.com;
www.glasgowloftapartment.co.uk;
www.max-servicedapartments.co.uk;
www.dreamhouseapartments.com;
www.hot-el-apartments.com

Below: the pool at the Crowne Plaza Glasgow (see p.125).

Index

Credits

Insight Great Breaks Glasgow
Written by: Ron Clark, Colin Hutchison
and Nick Bruno
Updated by: Zoe Ross
Commissioning Editor: Rebecca Lovell
Picture Researcher: Richard Cooke
Maps: APA Publications
Publishing Manager: Rachel Fox
Series Editor: Carine Tracanelli

All pictures by Douglas Macgilvray/APA
except: Abode Hotels 125; akg-images/
annanphotographs.co.uk 38B; Alamy 33T,
98; Axiom 81T; Murray Barnes 121B; Mike
Beltzner 16T; Bruno Bord 59; Tom Brogan
11, 122T; Crawford Brown/Rex Features 40;
Cornell Univeristy Library 8T; Citizens Theatre
Ltd 34T; David Cruickshanks/APA 4BL, 5TL,
9, 25B, 28T, 29B, 41, 45, 54T&B, 57T, 58B,
62, 64B, 69L&R, 80B, 103, 104T&B, 123T;
Jean-Pierre Dalbéra 88T, 94T, 96B; Elspeth
Durkin 36B; Epic Scotland 46/47; Dreamstime
2/3, 5ML, 72BL, 75, 76, 77; Fotolia 117T;
fotoLibra 5TR&BL, 100T, 106/107, 107, 113;
Getty Images 66/67, 66T; Giant Productions
Ltd 31B; Glasgay! Festival 123B; Glasgow City
Marketing Bureau 43B, 111, 116T, 118T;
Glasgow Film Festival 10B; Stéphane Goldstein
55T&B; David Grinly 4BR; Paul Hart 105;
Hotel du Vin 124; Hunterian Museum and Art
Gallery, University of Glasgow 78B, 79T&B,
80T; iStockphoto.com 4TR, 5CR, 18B, 19T&B,
20T, 21T, 22/23(all), 24T&B, 26, 27, 30B,
33B, 35B, 36/37, 38T&C, 51, 52B, 56R, 70T,
71B, 76, 86T, 87B, 101, 108/109(all), 110,
116B, 118B, 119, 121T, 122B; Ilpo Koskinen
60; Leonardo 126; Library of Congress
52T; John Lindie 17B, 82B, 84, 87T; James
Macdonald 5CL, 32B; Graeme Maclean 117B;
Seth Mcanespie 44B; Raymond McCrae 86B;
Jim McDougall 90T, 91; Alistair McMillan 112B;
Photolibrary 12/13, 63T, 102, 112T; Pictures
Colour Library 38/39, 48, 114/115; Sheep
Purple 25T; Colin Reilly 14; Stuart Reynolds/
Rex Features 50; John Robertson 44T; Paul
Robertson 37B; Scottish Viewpoint 34B, 99;

Scottish Youth Theatre 47B; stevecadman on
Flickr 46B, 49, 61; Nigel Swales 106B; Stephen
Thomas 89B; Topfoto 42B, 90B; Ville.fi 43T;
Nesbit Wylie 63B.
Cover pictures by: (front) Superstock (T),
Fotolia (BL) & iStockphoto (BR); (back)
Douglas Macgilvray/APA (T); Dreamstime.

CONTACTING THE EDITORS: As every
effort is made to provide accurate information
in this publication, we would appreciate it
if readers would call our attention to any
errors and omissions by contacting:
Apa Publications, PO Box 7910,
London SE1 1WE, England.
insight@apaguide.com

Worldwide distribution enquiries:
APA Publications GmbH & Co. Verlag KG
(Singapore Branch), 7030 Ang Mo Kio Ave 5,
08-65 Northstar @ AMK, Singapore 569880
apasin@signet.com.sg

Distributed in the UK and Ireland by:
Dorling Kindersley Ltd (a Penguin Company)
80 Strand, London, WC2R 0RL, UK
sales@uk.dk.com